THE RADIUM WOMAN

THE RADIUM WOMAN

A Life of Marie Curie

by ELEANOR DOORLY

and Woodcuts by
ROBERT GIBBINGS

ROY PUBLISHERS, NEW YORK

LIBRARY OF CONGRESS CATALOG CARD NUMBER: 54–10466

PRINTED IN GREAT BRITAIN
AT THE WINDMILL PRESS
KINGSWOOD, SURREY

To
VICTORIA DE BUNSEN

CONTENTS

Frontispiece, by Robert Gibbings

Author's Foreword

CHAPTER I

Manya Singing

WHY not? Why not? *Why* not? Why shouldn't Manya be allowed to read? She didn't ask the question. She would not think of asking her gentle, beautiful mother why not; she only puzzled her own little stubborn head where a pair of bright, grey-blue eyes looked penetratingly out from under a shock of yellow hair.

It was always like that! She had only to say: "Mayn't I read?" or to put out a hand towards a book and someone would be sure to say: "Manya dear, run into the garden" or "You haven't been to see your doll all day" or "Build me a house with those lovely new blocks." Manya knew all their wiles. Reading was naughty—naughty for her, but not for Bronia; and yet she could read and Bronia couldn't. It was very puzzling and apparently all the fault of the day when she had snatched a book from Bronia. She hadn't meant anything wrong. Bronia had asked her to play with the cardboard letters when they had nothing to do in their uncle's orchard except lie on the grass and move the bits of cardboard into words. Then one day, after they came home, their father had said to Bronia: "Let's see how the reading has got on." Bronia had stood with the open book, spelling the words and stumbling over them. So

Manya had seized it from her and read! "Manya!" her mother had exclaimed, surprised and shocked and her father had looked solemn while Bronia had sulked. There had been nothing for Manya to do but to cry and sob out: "Beg pardon . . . Manya didn't mean it."

Since that day no reading had been allowed, so Manya stood hesitating at her mother's door wondering what she should do. All morning she had been carrying ammunition for Bronia across the long dormitory floor in the great war against Joseph's and Hela's fort. The fort was built of the new blocks and the ammunition consisted of blocks also and she had grown too hot and tired, so that game had been stopped as far as she was concerned. There was nothing for it but to find her elder sister and go into the garden. "Zosia! . . . Zosia!" she called through the house and the two went off hand in hand. Zosia was twelve and almost grown up in the eyes of the other four, who were Joseph, Hela, Bronia, aged eight, and Manya. Manya was four when she learned to read and five on the day we are talking about, which explains why she was not allowed to read. Monsieur and Madame Sklodovski did not want their clever little girl pressed. But it had not occurred to them to tell her the reason.

The garden was big, level and walled in, with a rather worn grass patch and lots of trees. In much of it they could play to their hearts' content, but they had to be careful what they did on their way out and in, because they had to pass the windows of an Ogre. The garden belonged to the boys' High School, and in the school both the Sklodovskis and the Ogre lived. Even Zosia was nervous when she had to pass those windows and lowered her voice to a whisper, telling her little sister to be quite silent while they tip-toed past.

Although she was only five, Manya already knew quite a number of things. She knew that the Ogre was an ogre because he belonged to the people who had cut her own country into three parts and shared them out, like a giant dividing his spoil with two other giants. She was a Polish child and the ogre was the Russian Director of the school in which her father taught Mathematics and Physics. He was there to see that all the Polish men, women and children pretended properly to be Russian and Manya knew that with such people you had to be on your guard, careful and quiet so as not to be caught.

There was another thing that Manya knew very well: the country was a lovely place, though she lived in the town. In the country there were crowds and crowds and uncles and aunts and cousins; there was a stream to paddle in and mud to make mud pies and plenty of sun to cook the delectable cakes. There was the old lime tree that seven cousins sat in, eating gooseberries from cool cabbage leaves. When she appeared they would hoist her up to their crooked perch and make a collection for her from each of the seven cabbage leaves. In July, Manya was a wild little peasant.

Then there was her mother. Manya knew that she loved her more than anything else in the world. She was very beautiful, so it was not surprising that Manya thought so, or that she loved her beautiful singing. She loved, too, her mother's odd little way of stroking her hair and her forehead when she went to bed, instead of kissing her and when, in the evening all the family knelt around the table and prayed "Pray God make our mother better," Manya never supposed it was because her mother was ill or that that had anything to do with not being kissed.

Manya had been born on November the 7th, 1867, and named Marya, but she was more often called Manya or Manyusia—or oftenest of all, a strange pet name, Anciupecio, for in Poland they love nicknames. Zosia had spent the time in the garden telling her a long story about Anciupecio, because Zosia told stories better than anybody else and often made up gay little plays which she acted for her brother and sisters, taking all the parts herself. So real were those plays that Manya used to laugh and shudder by turns and not be quite sure in which country she lived or who were the people next door or who the people in the story.

When they reached the house, they found that their father had just finished school and was sitting in his study, the largest, happiest room in the house. The two entered very quietly. There sat their mother making a pair of shoes for Manya. Creak, creak went the scissors, cutting through the hard leather. Snap, snap crackled the waxed thread as it tightened and grew taut between the layers, and clack, clack tapped the hammer on the nails. Madame Sklodovski's thin white hands were nimble and cunning even at such hard work as that—and they needed to be, because five children wear out a mighty deal of shoe leather in a year.

That evening their father was talking about the Ogre. He often talked about him. The Ogre meant much to the family and was going to mean more. He had recently punished a Polish boy savagely for making a grammatical mistake in Russian, which is one of the hardest of foreign languages, and Monsieur Sklodovski had not been able to resist the temptation of saying: "But you too, sir, though you are a Russian by birth, sometimes make a grammatical mistake in that language." The Ogre did not at once retort. He glowered and scowled, but he saved up his revenge for another year.

Manya wandered round her father's room, straight little nose in the air, dreamily thinking her own thoughts, touching her pet ornaments, keeping carefully from disturbing her brother and sisters, who were doing their homework around their father's big, flat-topped desk. Manya was not at all interested in the splendid picture of a bishop which hung on the wall; it was said to be by a famous painter, but that was not the kind of thing she liked. She loved the clock on the desk and stayed a long time peering into its face and listening to its loud tick, tock. Then she ran her fingers daintily along the smooth marble top of the many-coloured Sicilian table; she liked that too, but not the whatnot with its blue Sèvres cup. She drew herself carefully away from that as the thing was breakable and something terrible might happen if she touched it. Not so the next treasures; they were more friendly and more mysterious with lovely, long, incomprehensible names—the barometer hanging on the wall which her father examined and tapped so seriously every day under the children's watchful eyes; the glass cupboard containing glass tubes and delicate balances and minerals and a goldleaf electroscope. "What . . . ?" Manya began one day.

"What are those?" interrupted her father in a solemn, teasing voice, "Those are *physical apparatus.*"

Little did he think . . . ! Little did Manya think what was going to happen to her and physical apparatus, but she liked the odd sounding words and ran off chanting:

Phýs-ĭ-căl áp-păr-á-tús.
Phýs-ĭ-căl áp-păr-á-tús.

CHAPTER II

Manya Learning

MANYA's school was an odd place and she learned odd things: how, for instance, to do what one is forbidden to do; how to hide one's disobedience quickly; how to seem to be doing what one isn't; how to diddle government inspectors; and because Manya was cleverer than most children, she was soon doing all these things better than the others. But the queerest thing of all in that school was that her form mistress and the headmistress found her a great help and not, as you might have thought, a great nuisance.

One day her class of twenty-five were having a delicious history lesson—a much more delicious history lesson than English children have ever had because it was a forbidden lesson. All the twenty-five and their mistress knew it was forbidden.

There they sat, the twelve year olds. Manya, aged only ten, was in the third row, near the high window looking out on to the snowy lawn. All the twenty-five were in navy blue with steel buttons and white collars, their hair tightly plaited and tied behind their ears with a neat tight bow. Their ears were all stretched, left ear listening hard for every word of history, right ear quick to catch the first tinkle of a certain door bell—conspirators all! Mistress and pupils were waiting, working, waiting to be caught!

Manya was in the middle of answering a question. . . . Her mistress liked her to answer as she was always top in history, top too in arithmetic, literature, German and French. On this occasion she was telling what she had learned of the Polish king, Stanislas Auguste.

"He was elected King of Poland," said she, "in 1764. He was a clever, highly educated king, a friend of poets and artists. He understood the causes of Poland's weakness and tried to make her strong, but alas, he had no courage. . ." Even Manya knew that a king should have courage and her voice was full of fierce regret, the fierce regret of a ten year old, who understood quite a lot. Tang—, tang—, ting, ting. Everybody shivered once. Everybody moved quickly, absolutely silently. Tupcia, as they called their mistress, piled her Polish books, every child piled her exercise books and her Polish history. The five whose duty it was, gathered all the books into their aprons and carried them with all speed to the boarders' bedrooms. The rest got out their needlework and were making exquisite buttonholes in cotton squares as if they had never done anything else.

The Russian inspector came in, accompanied by the unhappy headmistress, who had not been able to prevent his walking fast, and was in a panic lest the warning bell, with its two long rings and two short, had not given the children time to hide their disobedience. But there was no sign of anything but needlework, except that perhaps five little girls looked rather hot and breathless. But a man would not notice that.

Monsieur Hornberg, the inspector, sat down heavily. He was a fine looking man in spite of his fat and his shaved head. His uniform helped him with its yellow trousers and blue jacket fastened with well-polished silver buttons. In silence, he looked piercingly at the children through his gold-rimmed glasses and glanced swiftly at the book Tupcia had laid open on the desk with a bored air.

"You were reading aloud while they worked?" he questioned. "What is the book?"

"*Krylov's Fairy Tales.* We have just begun it to-day."

M. Hornberg knew that Russian book well and sincerely approved of it. He opened one of the desks and found it tidily empty. The button-holing had stopped and the children were politely waiting for his words of wisdom. It was not he who would have the eyes to see in their motionless faces the fear, the cleverness, the hatred that was there behind their solemn eyes.

"Mademoiselle, call up one of those young people, please."

Tupcia was relieved; she could choose one who would not make a hash of things. The one, however, was praying not to be called up. "Don't let it be me, God, *please* God. . . ." She did not hear God say: "Marya Sklodovska, the world is waiting for you to learn to do disagreeable things greatly." She did hear Tupcia call Marya Sklo-dovska!

She got up, turned hot, turned cold; shame clutched at her young throat.

"Say the Lord's Prayer," ordered Hornberg.

Manya obeyed, saying it in Russian as the foreign ruler bade, not in Latin, according to the custom of her own religion.

"Mention the Czars of Holy Russia since Catherine II."

"Catherine II, Paul I, Alexander I, Nicolas I, Alexander II," recited Manya in perfect Russian as if she had been born in St. Petersburg.

"And the names and titles of the Czar's family."

"Her Majesty, the Empress, His Imperial Highness, the Czarevitch Alexander, His Imperial Highness, the Grand Duke . . ."

"Good! Who governs us?"

Manya hesitated.

"Who governs us?" repeated the inspector, irritated.

"His Majesty, Alexander II, Czar of all the Russias," stammered Manya, turning pale.

The inspection was over and the inspector gone, very well satisfied with what he had seen and heard and feeling that he was making a real success of his department. But Manya broke down and cried as if her heart would break.

At the end of school, outside in the street, the excited children had a tale to tell their aunts and mothers and nurses who had come to fetch them;

but in whispers they told it, for they knew only too well that any passer-by, any lounger, might be a spy, who would repeat to the government what even a child said.

Hela and Manya took their Aunt Lucia by each arm. "The inspector questioned Manya," whispered Hela. "She answered like a brick, but cried like a baby afterwards. Anyway, the inspector hadn't any fault to find with anybody."

Manya held her tongue. She hated it all—hated being afraid, hated being made to feel that she belonged to an enslaved nation, hated having to lie, to lie all the time. As she clung to her aunt's arm, she remembered all the things she hated: the Ogre who had managed to turn her father out of his professorship. That had made them so that they were obliged to have students lodging in their house, which was horrid and often made them uncomfortable and unhappy. But that unhappiness was as nothing in comparison with not having Zosia any more, Zosia to tell her tales, Zosia to listen to all she had to say. Zosia had caught typhus from one of the students and had gone away for ever.

Across the sunny, snowy park the three made their way to the old town of Warsaw with its narrow streets and high, sloping-roofed houses ringed with snow. From unexpected corners, odd little sculptures looked out, Virgins' faces or strange stone animals.

Suddenly, the old church bells clanged out above their heads, clear and noisy in the frosty air. There were quite a crowd of churches just there and Aunt Lucia drew the children in through the dark door of one where they used to go to mass years before. How could Manya go in now, without Zosia? But she went in, because there was a colder fear than any other in her heart now and she wanted to persuade God to let her mother get better. "Let mother get better," she prayed. "Let me die instead of mother, *please*, God."

Out in the crisp winter air again Aunt Lucia had a treat to propose: they were to go down to the Vistula to buy the household apples from the market boats. Forgetting their sorrows, the children ran down the long steps that led to the river. The great Vistula rolled its yellowish, sombre vastness around low sandy islands, great empty barges slowly heaved against one another, sometimes thudding with a low sound into the floating baths and wash-houses at the bank. Only around the two long apple barges was there life in that winter season, for they had come from far up the river to bring red, rosy joy to children in Warsaw. The master, cosy in his sheepskin coat, swaying as he moved about the craft, lifted the straw here and there to show the purchasers how red and polished and free from frost his merchandise was in spite of its many days' journeying down the Vistula.

Hela first, then Manya threw down muff and satchel and began excitedly choosing their own apples, piling them in the great wicker basket that

was to carry them home, throwing any bad ones
they had the luck to find far far out into the river,
seeing who could throw the furthest.

Then Aunt Lucia engaged a boy to carry home
the basket and marched her charges off the boat,
each munching the reddest of all the apples.

At home at five o'clock, there was a meal of
something more substantial than apples and then
homework round the big desk. Soon a loud murmur rose from those aggravating people who do
lessons aloud, a trying custom in other lands besides Poland. Those children had to learn their
lessons in Russian. Mathematics in Russian for
Polish children were even harder than usual.
French and German grammar was all in Russian
and words they did not know had to be looked
up in Russian dictionaries. They might, of course,
explain their difficulties to themselves in Polish,
but when the next morning came they had to say
the lesson in Russian and to go through a geo-
metrical problem in a foreign language. They
had to write their essays in a tongue not their own
and to read French directly into Russian. Learning was a hard matter.

But Manya was a witch. She knew things by
magic without learning them; she had to read her
Russian verses only twice to know them without
a mistake, lucky scrap! But she was also a kind-
hearted scrap, for when her homework was done
under time, she would help other people through
their maze of difficulty. Not always, though. If
she got a chance, she would put a book between

her elbows on the table, her hands over her ears to keep out Hela's recitation, and . . . read! When Manya read, there was no waking her from her absorption; she heard nothing. A whole household might plan to tease and make a noise like all the zoos let loose with tin cans to play with and yet Manya wouldn't hear till her book was done. That was concentration and it was a joyful gift to have seized from the lucky-bag of life.

Once the others built a scaffolding of chairs round her as she read, a chair on each side, a chair behind and on top, three more chairs and so on over her head. She didn't hear or see a shadow of a chair or builder. She didn't hear delighted whispering or stifled laughter. When she had finished, she raised her head and down came the whole edifice amid shouts of laughter from the others. That didn't please Manya. She rubbed a bruised shoulder and went into another room, flashing at her elders as she passed just: "That's silly!"

When bedtime came, the Sklodovski girls slept on skins in the dining-room because the bedrooms had to be given to the students who paid. In the night the skins used to slip off and leave them cold. In the morning they had to get up in the dark because the dining-room had to be ready for the students' breakfast.

But such things as that were of no importance to Manya. Her mother was growing more and more i , even she could see that. She prayed to God a ways, but He seemed not to listen to ten year ol Manya. And in the spring, in May, before sh was eleven, her mother slipped away, whispe ing to her little girl: "I love you."

Man a was learning very much; was learning that life asks for courage from nations and men and children, not only from kings. She had thoughts of her own about it all. It seemed to her unjust and cruel and not at all to be understood. She was headstrong and angry and not at all submissive.

Chapter III

Rebels

MANYA at fourteen was not yet as pretty as her sisters. Bronia was quite grown up with long sweeping skirts and her golden hair done up into a bun at the back. She had taken her mother's place and looked after the housekeeping and the lodgers. Hela was sixteen and a beauty, fair and tall and graceful. Joseph was also fair and tall and handsome. He was at the university studying medicine.

The girls would have liked to think of themselves as going to the university also, but in Russian Poland no woman was allowed to go to any university. If they wanted to learn more than they learned at school, they had to g᛫ their learning from books for themselves or in an ᛫her country.

For the moment, Manya was content for he᛫ self. She had gone on to the High School and was as happy as a squirrel with all the nuts it needed; but she was worried about Bronia. What would Bronia do without a university? Couldn't she, Manya, invent a scheme to get Bronia to some country where girls could learn what they wanted to know? She made up her mind to work and earn money to keep her elder sister. Well, the high road to earning was to get through school successfully!

Manya, that particular morning, would be late
for school unless she finished breakfast quickly,
cut up the sandwiches for school lunch, saved, yes
saved, the meat from Lancet who had interrupted
her thoughts by a quick grab at the last of the
mutton which was waiting to be cut up for those
sandwiches. Lancet was the red setter, the adored
of the household. He was very beautiful and did
everything he shouldn't. He had golden feathers
on ears and tail and feet and should have been a
most obedient shooting dog, but he had had no
education. Manya, her brother and sisters spoilt
him all day, kissed him, even made a lap dog of
him. He slept in the chairs, brushed vases down
with his tail, ate other people's lunch, upset
visitors with his uproarious welcome, took their
hats and gloves for them with the politest air—
gloves and hats that looked sadly the worse for
wear when they were returned to their owners.

At last lunch having been safely wrapped
up, her satchel slung on her back and Lancet
persuaded to stay at home, Manya ran off to
school.

At the blue palace where Count Zamoyski
lived, she stopped, hesitated before the great
bronze lion guarding one of its old stone court-
yards and put her hand on the heavy ring in its
mouth to turn it over its nose.

"Don't run away, Manyusia," called a voice
from a window; "Kazia'll be there in a minute."
Manya always picked up Kazia, who was the
daughter of the Count's librarian, on her way to

school; but if her friend were late, she turned the bronze ring up and went on. Then Kazia could be in no doubt whether she had passed.

"Come to tea this afternoon," called Kazia's mother; "there'll be your favourite iced chocolate."

"Of course you're coming to tea," said Kazia. "Oh! Aren't we late? Come on!"

So the two hurried along the narrow street and through the park, neither of them conscious of the difference everyone else could see in them. Kazia was so well dressed, so obviously the petted daughter of two devoted parents, while Manya was a little left to herself, a little shabby.

It was a long way to school and they had plenty of time for chatter, time too to play certain games. In the wet weather they made a point of trailing their goloshes through the deepest parts of the puddles; in the dry, they played the "green" game.

"Do come to the shops and buy a new exercise book," said Manya. "I have seen some awfully jolly ones with green covers that will . . ."

But Kazia wasn't caught. At the word green and before Manya could finish her sentence she handed her a piece of green velvet she was keeping ready for the purpose in her pocket. She escaped a forfeit and for the moment nothing more followed. Manya seemed to have given up the game. She began talking about their last history lesson in which the professor had gone out of his way to tell them that Poland was a mere province of Russia and the Polish language a Patois.

"Still he seemed uncomfortable," she remarked. "Did you see that he dared not look at us and turned quite pale?"

"Yes!" said Kazia; "he was almost green." And immediately, she saw Manya twiddling a young green chestnut leaf under her nose.

"We've passed the monument!" a cry of horror from Manya. "Oh, well! We've got to go back"; and back they went right to Saxe Square where there was a lofty column supported by four lions. On it was written "To the Poles faithful to their Monarch." The Czars had erected the monument to those Poles who, traitors to their own country, had died fighting on the side of the oppressor. It had become the duty of all Poles who were faithful to Poland to spit at the monument every time they passed it and Manya and Kazia would not leave that duty undone even if it meant retracing their steps or being late for school.

"Are you coming to watch the dancing to-night?" asked Manya. Naturally Kazia was going. Every week a few families met to dance at the Sklodovskis; but only the girls who were "out" were allowed to dance. Kazia and Manya were obliged to sit still and watch. Nevertheless they were getting hints of how to do it, studying the steps, discussing the movements, learning the tunes; and when the grown-up dancing was over, they practised by themselves.

They were eagerly discussing the joys of

coming out as they walked under the school archway into the courtyard. Girls from every direction were trooping into the great bare, three-storied building; there were laughter and chatter and gaiety and many greetings. But one girl was hurrying in alone as if she wished to escape notice. As the two caught her up, they saw that her eyes were swollen and red and her clothes were untidy as if she had scrambled into them anyhow.

"What's the matter with Kunicka?" they asked one another and one of them slipped an arm round the girl.

"What's the matter, Kunicka?"

Kunicka could scarcely answer, her pale face was drawn with pain. "It's my brother," she stammered. "He's been caught in a plot. . . . For three days we hadn't had any news of him. . . . They're . . . they're going to hang him at dawn to-morrow."

The words seemed to have no meaning. The two drew Kunicka out of the crowd; bending over her, they tried to understand, tried to comfort her. But there was no comfort for someone whose brother was going to be hanged to-morrow! Manya and Kazia knew the young, gay brother. He was their friend. He had done nothing wrong. How could he be going to die?

"Make haste, children! Enough talking!" It was the hated voice of the German superintendent, Miss Mayer, and the three were obliged to bury their grief and go into school.

It was no longer the private school to which Manya had gone as a little girl, but the government High School, run by the Russian government. In it, everything except the pupils were Russian. The Polish children were obliged to attend it, because only by so doing could they get a certificate of any sort which would enable them to get work. They attended, but they were rebels and freer to express their opinions than their elders. Manya and Kazia took delight in inventing witticisms against their Russian professors, their German master and especially against Miss Mayer who detested Manya only a little less than Manya detested her.

Little and dark Miss Mayer used to go about in soft slippers not to be heard and the better to spy on the girls.

"It's no more use speaking to that Sklodovska girl," she said, "than throwing green peas at a wall!"

"Look at your ridiculous, frizzy, disorderly head, Marya Sklodovska! How often have you been told to confine your curls? Come here and let me brush them down and make you look like a decent school girl." "Like a German Gretchen!" thought Manya, but she said nothing. So with the brush that brushed everybody's hair, she set on Manya's head with good hard blows. But however hard she brushed, the curls were rebels still—those light, capricious, exquisite curls that framed Manya's round, rebellious face.

"I won't have you look at me like that!" Miss

Mayer would shout. "You have n   to look down on me!"

"I can't help it," said Manya truthfully, for she was a head taller than Miss Mayer. No doubt she was glad that words sometimes have two meanings.

But the girls liked some of their teachers, for some were Polish. In some of the Russians also, to their dumb surprise, they found Polish sympathies. They began to understand that even in Russia there were rebels. One Russian master had gone so far as to give as a prize a book of revolutionary poems. That silent act became the talk of the school and the pupils watched him with wondering, admiring eyes. Poles could live with Russians. Oh, yes! Were not the pupils in that city school Russians, Poles, Germans, Jews? And were they not all happy together? In school they found no difference in the races. Outside school each nation kept apart, for all feared spies.

In spite of everything Manya loved her school; a little shamefacedly she confessed it. "Do you know, Kazia," she wrote one holiday, "I like the school. Are you going to laugh at me? I like it. I even like it very much. I am not longing for it. No! But I am not sad at the thought of term and two years more of it is no horrible thought."

But on that particular day, when Miss Mayer called the girls in from the courtyard, Manya had no thought for school. In the sunny morning, she had been dreaming of music and dance and jesting. Suddenly the world had changed. While the

dim words of unheard lessons floated around her
ears, she could see nothing but the young eager
boy whom she knew . . . and a cold, pictured
dawn with a gallows.

There was no thought of dancing at the Sklodovskis that night. Manya, Bronia and Hela,
Kazia and Ula, her sister, all went to sit up the
night through with Kunicka, keeping watch in the
long night, thinking of the boy who had to die.
That keeping watch is a Catholic custom, it is
just staying awake to think. The six children sat
with Kunicka. We who are happier cannot
imagine what they thought or felt. It is so different when someone we love dies naturally, even
children understand that; but this other—to sit
and wait while the minutes pass and the hour of
man's exceeding cruelty comes nearer to stain the
dawn with wrong—that was horror indeed. They
must have watched in silence, for there was
nothing to say, nothing to do, only plenty to think,
rebel thoughts for the hearts of six young rebels.
From time to time, they did what they could for
Kunicka, their own hearts breaking with sympathy. They tried to get her to drink something
warm; gently they put their arms around her or
tried to dry her tears. Then suddenly they realised that the new light was no longer candlelight.
There was a red line in the sky. The red dawn
had come. The six buried their terrified faces in
their hands and threw themselves on their knees
to pray for the young rebel who was dead.

CHAPTER IV

A Whole Year's Holiday

MANYA was sixteen. Gold medal day had come and Manya's gold medal was the third in the family. It was June and very hot. Manya, like all the prize winners, was dressed in black with a bunch of tea roses in her belt. The crowd pressed around her congratulating her and shaking hands. When it was all over, she left the High School for good, her fingers pressed tight on her proud father's arm.

He had promised her a whole year's holiday. That was a gift indeed, a year's holiday! Manya hadn't an idea why she should have it, but her father thought that as she had been working very hard and as she had done her work in less time than other girls, it was only fair that she should take that delightful way of waiting for her age-fellows to catch her up. So Manya the industrious became a lazy-bones and entered into the full fun of the thing.

"My dear little Devil," she wrote to Kazia, "I don't believe algebra and geometry exist. Anyway I have completely forgotten them. I don't even do my embroidery. I don't do anything. I get up at ten, or sometimes at six—in the morning, be it spoken—I read nothing or only tales. I am the stupidest of the stupid and I laugh all alone at my complete inanity. A crowd of us wander through the woods or play battledore and shuttlecock, at which I am a booby, or puss-in-the-corner or follow-my-leader or any such intellectual game. Wild strawberries are everywhere and for a penny-farthing we can buy enough for a meal—that's a soup-plate full, piled high and overflowing. Alas! Alas! they are almost over and my appetite is limitless so that I am quite scared at my greed. We swing . . . we swing right up into the sky. We bathe, we catch shrimps by torchlight. By-the-bye, we have met an actor. He sang to us and recited to us and gathered us so many gooseberries that in return we plaited him a crown of wild poppies and white pinks and blue cornflowers and threw it at him as he left for Warsaw. They say he put it on and then, when the train came in, packed it in his suitcase and took it all the way to the city."

Manya was to spend her year in the country. She loved every bit of it. She was to watch all the seasons go round and to discover at every turn fresh beauties in the land of Poland. Her uncle, Xavier, lived on the plains of Zwola. There she looked over level land to the furthest, furthest horizon of which one could dream, green land streaked with the brown colours of ploughed earth. Her uncle had many horses in stable and there she learned to ride. What she wore didn't matter to her. She borrowed trousers from her cousin which were too big for her, turned them up, belted them into gathers and was ready. Left hand on reins and holding the big horse's mane, left foot in the stirrup and right hand on the saddle, she stood for the first adventure as she had seen her uncle and cousins stand. But what a long way it was up! She would never get there however much she hopped or however still the good old horse stood.

"Good to try!" said her uncle, "scramble!" But her cousins did not leave her untaught. They showed her how to stand with her back to the horse's head before she sprang, how to help herself with a convenient mound and, finally, how to get just the right spring that could land her into the saddle of the tallest horse. It became her delight to go long expeditions on horseback over the spreading fields. Soon she could rise in the saddle at the trot or sit tight at the gallop. She explored new villages and met strange country folk and knew more and more of the Polish plain.

But an even greater pleasure was in store for her: she went to stay with another uncle, whose

name is quite unpronounceable to English ears, Uncle Zdzislaw, who lived among the Carpathian Mountains. For the first time she saw snowy heights, dazzling in their whiteness and dark pine forests like rivers of ink making the snow more white. . . . She longed to get closer up; to make her way through the trees, perhaps to the edge of the snow itself. She went for long walks up winding mountain paths which sometimes ended unexpectedly in a precipice, so that she had to retrace her steps. Sometimes the path ended at a hut and Manya and her cousins would go in and ask to see the owner's work; for all the mountaineers of that district were wood carvers and their simplest piece of furniture was a work of art. The peasants loved to show the things that they had made and when the children had admired the chairs and table and cuckoo clock and the coloured wooden bowls against the wall, they delved into cupboards and brought out little carved men or drinking cups or toys or even pictures carved in wood.

Once, in her wanderings, Manya came to a little mountain lake, a patch of water lying in the hills as blue as massed speedwell, and men called it "The sea's eye." It was so lovely lying among the snow peaks that Manya thought it the gem of the whole country.

Within doors, life was quite riotously merry. Her uncle loved gaiety; so did his beautiful wife and as to his three daughters, they laughed all day and Manya with them. Guests arrived in plenty.

Uncle and aunt would probably have been out shooting and have plenty of game to offer them. If they hadn't, there was nothing to do but slay a barn door chicken of which there were hundreds running about the yard. Then the girls flew to the kitchen and hastily baked the cakes. All was ready for the feast. For clothes, they hastily turned out cupboards and sewed together gay fancy dresses for charades, or if it was winter, for a "Kulig"—a winter fête.

Manya's first Kulig was a tremendous experience. The night was dark, but lit by the strange northern snow-light. Manya and her three cousins, wrapped in thick rugs, masked and dressed as Cracovian peasants, took their places in two sledges. Their outriders were boys in rustic costumes who lit the darkness with fantastic torches. Through the dark forest, they caught glimpses of other torches approaching. The cold night was suddenly filled with music, for the musicians were coming up, bringing four little Jews, who for two whole nights and two whole days were to wring heart-stirring airs from their violins. They would play waltzes and mazurkas and all the world would catch up the refrains and sing them in chorus, making the night tuneful and noisy.

As the Jews played, other sledges joined them out of the darkness, three, five, ten sledges. In spite of hair-raising bends and glassy slopes those little musicians never missed a note as they led the fantastic troop under the frosty stars.

At the first lone farmhouse the sledges stopped with jingling bells and harness and all the com-

pany, laughing, shouting, and knocking loudly on the door, awakened the inmates, who were only pretending to be asleep. In a few moments the musicians were hoisted on to a table and the ball began in a room lit by torches.

Presently supper was brought and then, at a signal, suddenly the whole house was empty—empty of casks, of inhabitants, of horses, of sledges, of everything. A larger procession, with all the sledges of the new homestead, was wending its way through the forest to another farm.

A sledge with fresh horses, trying to pass another, went out of the beaten road, failed to get back and overturned in the snowdrift. The procession halted, torches waving in the wind, and gathered into a semicircle while willing hands brushed the snow from the occupants and righted their sledge. Again the bells rang out a wild peal of jingling speed in the night. But what had become of the musicians? Nobody knew. The leading sledge went faster and faster, hoping to catch them up; but it was soon apparent that they were not on that road; they had not gone on! A halt was called, a fork in the road was remembered. There was nothing for it but to go back and look, for the little Jews along the other road. Everyone was worried. How would the dance go at the other farms if the musicians could not be found? But presently someone caught the joyful cry of violins above the sound of bells and the procession was complete again and growing in length as they stopped to dance at yet another farmhouse, and yet another and another.

The sun rose . . . the sun went down . . . the sun rose. The fiddlers had scarcely any time to eat or sleep. On the second night the vast train of sledges stopped with snorting horses and jingling bells before the biggest homestead for the real ball.

The little fiddlers played louder. The guests took their places for the famous figure dances. The chief boy, handsome and elegant, in his embroidered white costume advanced to lead out the best dancer of all the company. It was Manya Sklodovska, in the dress of a mountain maiden with a velvet jacket, puffed linen sleeves and a star-like crown decked with long, brightly coloured streamers.

They danced through the night. They danced a mazurka at eight in the morning. Manya said that never in her life had she enjoyed herself so much and her aunt said that if she enjoyed Kuligs so much, she should have one to celebrate her wedding.

But the joys of holidays were not over. An old pupil of Madame Sklodovska's, who had become Countess of Fleury, invited Hela and Manya to stay with her. The house stood on a tongue of land between two rivers. Manya had a lovely view from her room across the meeting waters and there she learned to row. "We do anything," she wrote home, "that comes into our heads. We sleep all night and sometimes in the day. We dance. We are mad. In fact only a lunatic asylum would suit us!"

They varied their sleeping and dancing with riding and mushroom gathering and practical jokes. Once Manya asked the Countess's brother to go to town on a message. The unsuspecting young man went. The town was far. He came home in the dark and went to his room where all the young people of the house had slung his bed, his table, his chairs, his trunks, his clothes from the beams of the roof. His possessions had become entirely aerial and slapped him in the face as he moved among them.

On another day, lunch had been prepared for distinguished guests and the children were not invited. They ate the whole lunch before lunch and placed, by the empty table, a scarecrow representing a most satisfied and well-fed count! The culprits? Where were they? Vanished into thin air!

On the anniversary of the Count and Countess's wedding day, the gay company sent them, by two of their number, a huge crown made of vegetables. It weighed a hundred pounds and was presented to the happy couple as they sat on a decorated throne. Then the youngest member recited a poem which had been written by Manya for the occasion and ended thus:

> For Louis' blessed day
> A picnic be our pay!
> For every girl invite a boy
> In your example let us joy
> And follow to the altar soon.
> Grant us, grant us now this boon!

The Count and Countess did their best with a ball instead of a picnic. Manya and Hela wanted to be especially ravishing that night. They were poor and their ball dresses well worn. They counted their money. They turned the dresses over and over. They ripped off the faded tulle and found the linings quite good. A little blue tarlatan would do, they decided, instead of the tulle, and a ribbon here, a ribbon there would create new dresses. Thin purses and a skilful needle would do wonders. Flowers would do the rest and there would be money enough for two new pairs of shoes. When the shopping was done and the needlework was done and the garden had done its share, the mirror said: "You'll do."

And Manya danced her new shoes through and fêted the morning by throwing them away.

CHAPTER V

People

MANYA was back in Warsaw. Her big grey eyes
looked out with a laugh in them at a changed
world. Her firm upper lip often twitched with a
merry smile, but her face was often serious. Like
the fathers of most of the world, Mr. Sklodovski
let his children know that they had their living to
earn. He had given up taking students and the
family again lived in a little house of their own.
It was hard enough, while their father was still
earning, to pay the rent, the daily girl and the
house-keeping and they had to look forward to
the time when he would have nothing but a
teacher's small pension to live on. That worried
him. Like the fathers of most of the world, he had
hoped to make enough money to provide for his
family. Sitting by the lamp in the evening, he
would sigh deeply. Four pair of happy eyes,
between periwinkle-blue and grey, would look up
at him and guess his thought; his four children
would all protest together: "Don't worry, Father,
aren't we all young and strong and able to earn
for ourselves?" Mr. Sklodovski must have wondered, as he smiled at their eagerness, whether
they would succeed in life as he had not done. He
had worked hard and been very gifted and yet
had won very little reward in money from life.

Would his children be like him? The bald-headed, short, fat, little man sat under the lamp in his dark, meticulously brushed, shabby coat. Everything about him was precise and neat: his handwriting, his thoughts, his expressions, even his actions. He had brought up his children with the same exquisite, neat care. When he took them on excursions he made out the itinerary before-hand, pointed out the beauties of the landscape to them, realising, perhaps, what few people know, that most people miss seeing beauty because no-body mentions it. If they came to an old or famous building, he would tell them its history. Manya saw no faults in her father. It never occurred to her to mock his precise little ways. She thought of him as a fount of universal know-ledge. And, indeed, he knew many things. He kept up with the new discoveries in physics and chemistry by buying learned pamphlets with his hard-earned savings. He knew, without a thought of his own cleverness, Greek and Latin and five modern languages. He wrote verse and read aloud beautifully to his children every Saturday even-ing so that they grew to know great literature. When he wanted to read to them some foreign book, *David Copperfield*, for example, he read it in Polish though the copy in his hand was English.

"There's nothing new at home," wrote Manya to a friend. "The plants are quite well, thank you! The azaleas are in flower and Lancet is asleep on the rug! I have had my dress dyed and Gucia, the daily maid, is altering it. She's just

done Bronia's, which is a success. I have little
time and still less money. A lady who was recom-
mended to us for lessons came; but when Bronia
told her they would cost her a shilling an hour,
she fled as if the house were on fire."

Yet, paid badly or not, Manya had to teach.
Nothing else was open to girls in those days. But
she didn't think: "How many pupils can I get?
What can I earn?" That wasn't Manya! She had
her dreams—not the girl dream of getting
married, nor the boy dream of engine driving.
Her dream was Poland. She, Manya Sklodovska,
must help Poland. How could she do *that* with
her sixteen years and the stuff her father and her
school and books had put into her head? There
were others who dreamed for Poland, Manya
knew, and plotted to throw bombs at the Czar.
There were those who dreamed that God would
answer their prayers for Poland. But, though
Manya lent her passport to a revolutionary, she
dreamed neither of those dreams. She believed
that the most practical dream is the best: do the
thing that is just in front of you; teach the Poles
whom the Russian government was doing its best
to keep ignorant; teach and teach and teach till
Warsaw should become a great centre for the
things of the mind, till Poland should lead Europe
by being best.

New ideas were spreading in England and
France. Manya had a friend ten years older than
herself who had got wind of them and had started
a secret society called the "Winged University" to

study them. Manya, Bronia and Hela joined it.
The little company met at one another's houses to
be taught, not some weird or wild study, but just
anatomy, biology and natural history. Yet at the
sound of a knock at the door, a mouse in the
wainscot, everyone started and trembled. If the
police had caught them, it would have been prison
for everybody. The members had to teach as well
as learn. Manya collected a little library of books

to lend to poor people but she had to teach them
their letters and how to read before the books
could be of any use to them.

Sometimes a Polish shop would be glad to let
its work girls gather after work to meet Manya
and sit thumbing books and racking brains in
order to become more worthy citizens of Poland.
No one was afraid that a single girl would give
the secret away. Gay, reserved, little Manya,
among the older, rougher girls refused to allow a
single slang word or a single cigarette. Finding
her curls too attractive, she cut them off, not
noticing that by so doing she made herself look
still more childish. She was full of work, trying
her hand at everything: lectures, meetings, drawing, writing poetry, reading the literature of half

a dozen countries—above all, following the far thoughts of great writers.

But what occupied her thoughts most was what was she going to do with Bronia. Bronia was getting old, or at least so thought Manya, and no one would see to Bronia's career if she didn't. Morning after morning, in fair weather or foul, she went to give her paid lessons. The rich kept her waiting, to them she was just a poor teacher, in a draughty corridor. "So sorry, Miss Sklodovska, my little girl is late this morning; you'll be able to give her her full lesson, of course?" At the end of the month her pay was forgotten. "So sorry, my husband will pay the two months together." But Manya was needing the money then. She had been longing for it to buy a few necessary things.

Bronia was looking pale and discouraged. Manya would have to set aside her own ambitions, her desire to go to a university to satisfy her great need of knowledge. She must get Bronia off her hands first.

"Bronia, I have been thinking it all out," she said one day; "and I have spoken to father. I think I have found a way."

"A way to what?"

Manya had to be very careful and tactful. "Bronia, how long could you live in Paris on what you've saved?"

"I could pay the journey and one year's living, but Medicine needs five years," answered Bronia quickly.

"Yes, and lessons at a shilling an hour won't take us far."

"Well?"

"Well, if each of us is working for herself, neither of us will succeed. Whilst with my plan you can take your train this autumn."

"Manya! You're mad!"

"No. At first you can spend your own money and afterwards I will send you some. So will father. I can save for myself at the same time. And when you are a doctor, it will be my turn to go and you can help me."

There were tears in Bronia's eyes for she understood what the offer meant to Manya but she thought the arithmetic a little odd. "How are you going to keep yourself, to help me and to save all at the same time?" she asked.

"Ah! That's the *way* I am finding. I am going to get a resident post where I shall be kept by someone else and have no chance to spend anything! Isn't that perfect?"

"No," said Bronia, "I don't see why I should go first. You are cleverer. If you go first, you will succeed quickly and afterwards I can go."

"*Why?* Oh foolish Bronia, dear! Aren't you twenty and I only seventeen? You have been waiting centuries. I have time. The eldest must go first. When you have a practice, you can shower gold on me! Besides I have set my heart on it, so there!"

So in September, just a month before her eighteenth birthday, Manya found herself in the

D

waiting room of the Governesses' agency, dressed as she was sure a governess should be dressed. Her hair which had grown again was neatly done under her faded hat; her dress was plain and severe; everything about her was ordinary and quiet.

Nervously she approached the lady at the desk, holding her certificate and testimonials very tight. The lady read the testimonials very attentively and then suddenly looked at Manya; she even stared at her. "You really mean that you know German, Russian, French, Polish and English perfectly?" she questioned.

"Yes" said Manya, "though my English is not so good as the others. Still, I can teach it up to examination standard. I won the High School gold medal."

"Ah! And what salary do you want?"

"Forty pounds a year resident."

"I will let you know if a post offers." With that not-too-encouraging promise, Manya left the agency.

It was not long before Manya found herself a private governess. The family's name is secret, because they would not like to remember the trick fate played them. They opened a little door for Manya Slodovska, aged eighteen, and through it, as she tells us, she caught a little glimpse of hell and she wouldn't go through. Life meant Manya to be a great giver of gifts, not an unhappy, little despised slave. They were rich, the B—s; they kept the governess in her place, speaking to her as an iceberg might speak, could it creak out its thoughts. They threw their great wealth about in public, but they kept her six months without her salary and expected her not to read in the evenings in order to save lamp oil. Their speech to people's faces was honeysweet, but behind their backs so backbiting that Manya says they didn't leave their friends a dry thread to cover them.

"I have learnt from them," she wrote, "that people in books are true and that one is wise not to mix with those whom wealth has spoilt." Perhaps it was such knowledge, won when she was eighteen, that made Manya Sklodovska in the far future unspoilable by any offer of great wealth!

But Manya's plan was not working. Living at the B—s in town, she found that she spent a little money every day. It was very pleasant to be able to see her father sometimes and to be able to keep up with her friends of the winged university, but when you have made up your mind to a plan, you must carry it out whatever the cost. Manya found that she must leave home entirely, must get a post in the depth of the country, where she would be able to spend nothing. In that way, Bronia, who was already in Paris, would be able to have what she had planned for her.

The very post she was seeking turned up. It was far away in the country and it was a little better paid—fifty pounds a year this time. And, of course, fifty pounds went farther in those days than now. But it was with rather a sinking heart that Manya showed her new address to her father, though probably it did not look as outlandish and far away to him as it does to us.

Melle Marya Sklodovska
c/o Monsieur Z—
SZCZUKI,
near PRZASNYSZ

It was January when Manya set out for the country, a January in Poland where the snow lay thick for months together. As the train drew slowly out of the station, she realised that she could no longer see her father waving to her. For the first time in her life she was wholly alone and frightened. Those new people in a far away village, from which there was no escape might prove to be as unkind as her last employers. Or her father, who was getting old, might be taken ill. Ought she to have left him? The long fields of snow crept by in the gathering darkness, but they had long been blotted out by Manya's tears.

Three hours in the train and then a sledge to meet her. Warm fur rugs were tucked around her and out into the snowy majesty of the winter night she speeded through a silence broken only by the noise of sleigh bells.

Four hours in the sleigh. Iced and hungry, Manya wondered if the horses would ever stop. Then a yawning space of light, an open door and a whole family to meet her—the tall master of the house, the mistress, the shy children clinging to their mother's skirt, their eyes alive with curiosity. Madame welcomed her with warm, friendly words, gave her boiling tea, took her herself to her room, and left her alone to recover some warmth and to unpack her few shabby cases.

· · · · ·

Manya was in the depth of the country. She looked round with satisfaction at her white-washed, simply furnished room, with its warm stove in an alcove.

The next morning she drew her curtains, expecting to see snowy fields and forests bending under snow. Instead she was greeted with factory chimneys belching black smoke. She drew back and looked again—not one chimney but many, and not a tree to be seen, not a bush, not a hedge. She was in the sugar beet district. As far as the eye could see there was nothing but ploughed land waiting for beetroot. The whole country was devoted to beetroot. For beetroot the peasants ploughed and sowed and harvested. The factories were beetroot refineries. The village consisted of the cottages of the beetroot workers sheltering under factory walls. The house where she lived belonged to the director of beetroot. The river flowed coloured with beetroot.

The factories were a disappointment to Manya. So were the young men and maidens of the big houses round. They talked of nothing but what he said and she said, of the clothes they would wear, of who was giving the next ball and of how long the last had gone on. Manya was so horrified when Mr. and Mrs. Z— came home from a dance at one o'clock in the afternoon that she seemed to have forgotten how much she had once rejoiced at dancing till eight in the morning. "Give me the pen of a caricaturist," she exclaimed, "for some of these people are really worthy of it. The girls are geese, who don't know how to open their mouths and so far my Bronka, the eldest daughter of the house, is a rare pearl for sense and interest in life." Besides Bronka, there was another interesting person at Szczuki, her little brother Stas, aged three. He was the life of the long, one-storied house. His pattering feet went everywhere, down the long corridors, out into the glass verandahs that looked shabby under the leafless virginia creeper. His prattle amused Manya. Once his Nanny told him that God was everywhere. "Stas doesn't like that," he replied; "I'm afraid he'll catch me! Will he bite me?"

Andzia, Manya's special pupil, was ten and a Fidgetty Phyllis, who ran away from her lessons whenever a visitor called. Manya was supposed to teach her for four hours a day, but what with her perpetual running away and being caught and brought back and having to go back to the beginning again, work did not get on, as one might say, fast. Andzia, too, was apt to lie in bed till Manya pulled her out by the arm, a proceeding that aggravated Manya particularly. On one of those mornings, it took her two hours to recover her temper. The best part of her day were the three hours in which she read with Bronka and those other hours of leisure when she wrote long letters home: "I am coming to Warsaw at Easter," she said; "and at that thought everything in me rejoices so much that it is all I can do not to shout like a savage."

Along the muddy village lanes, she met the village children, dirty little boys and girls, their bright eyes looking out at her from under their matted tow-like hair. "Aren't these Poles?" she said to herself. "I, who have vowed to enlighten the people, can I not do something for them?" Those ragamuffins either had never learnt anything or only knew the Russian alphabet. Manya thought that it would be fun to start a secret Polish school for them.

Bronka was delighted when she heard of the idea. "Not so fast," said Manya. "If we are caught, it will be Siberia for us, you know." They both knew what Siberia meant—exile in a terrible land of frozen plains. But Bronka was ready to take the risk. The two girls obtained the permission of Mr. Z— and the class began.

Fortunately, there was an outside staircase to Manya's room. Ten or eighteen small, grubby boys and girls began to tramp up it. Manya borrowed a deal table and some benches and spent some of her valuable savings on buying exercise books and pens for her pupils. Then the fun began. Clumsy fingers grasped the unaccustomed instruments and letters were scrawled on white paper. Slowly the mysterious fact that you can

write the sounds you hear in black on white began
to dawn on the urchins. The proud parents, who
could not themselves read, came up the wooden
stairs and stood overwhelmed and delighted at
the back of the room watching the marvellous
thing a son or a daughter was doing. The sons
and daughters were not doing it easily. They
twisted, they sniffed, they groaned as if making a
letter was as hard as carrying beetroots up a
mountain. Manya and Bronka moved among
them, helping them in their painful trying. They
were smelly, they were often inattentive, they
weren't very clever, but for the most part, their
bright eyes showed that they were excited about
their lessons and longing to learn.

CHAPTER VI
Fortunate Misfortune

OTHER people's holidays come when the summer comes; but a governess stays at her post most of the year. She is even more useful when the boys come home, and little girls need getting out of bed winter and summer. Manya was bored. Nothing ever happened. To-morrow was always twin sister to yesterday—work from eight to half-past eleven, work from two to half-past seven, walk and lunch from half-past eleven to two. In the evening, it was reading aloud to Andzia if she had been good; sewing and talking if she had not. At nine o'clock at last came freedom to read her own books and to study. But even then she was liable to be interrupted to do one of the hundred and one things required of a governess. For instance, Andzia's godfather needed someone to play chess with him and the governess would do quite well; or a fourth was wanted at whist and it did not matter if the governess liked whist or not. Manya grew hungrier for knowledge as the chance of it slipped farther and farther away. Her books were old fashioned and there was no one with whom she could discuss her difficulties. She hadn't an idea what she was going to do. She thought with envy of the thousands of girls flocking to colleges the world over, meeting the choice and master spirits of their age, being taught and working in laboratories. Vienna, Berlin, London, St. Petersburg, especially Paris, seemed so many Meccas to her! No, not Vienna, Berlin or St. Petersburg for they were the capitals of Poland's oppressors. But London and Paris! She was wild with longing to go to Paris, free generous Paris that oppressed no one, but welcomed exiles and invited everyone to come to her who wanted to think, who wanted to know. Despair was getting hold of Manya. It was so hard to work alone. Her money accumulated so intolerably slowly and Bronia would need help for so many years. Her father also would be wanting her to take care of him when he was really old. Would Manya ever get to the university?

She had grown deliciously pretty. Her broad, lofty brow had all the sternness taken from it by her ravishing, burnished hair; her grey eyes deep-set under well-marked eyebrows seemed very large and gazed at one with gay and penetrating understanding; her wilful mouth with a suggestion of a smile forced one to look and think twice. Her skin was like a very peach. She was graceful, with exquisite wrists and ankles; and best of all her thoughtfulness gave her just that touch of mystery which makes people always want to know a girl.

Casimir, the eldest son of the house, was glad to find Manya there when he came home for the holidays. He came across her snipping off dead roses in the lovely garden. He had heard about her from his sister's letters, but he hadn't believed in her, and didn't he know all about the whole dull race of governesses?

"But. . . . By the sword of Poland!" he exclaimed to himself, "This one is different!"

"You have given your ragged school a holiday this morning, Mademoiselle?"

"Oh, no!" said Manya, her face alive with interest as usual. "They don't come till five, when their other work, whatever it may be, is done."

So, thought Manya, this was Bronka's adored brother, this tall, handsome, charming-mannered student, who spoke to her so friendlily and went on to take so lively an interest in her pupils whom he would insist on calling her "ragged school."

That evening she did not go at nine to her heavy books. There was far more to be learnt by real talk with a university student about the subjects he was studying. To-morrow lost its resemblance to yesterday. Summer broke the order of work. Casimir insisted on boating picnics and Manya was especially good at the oar. She rode so that it was a delight to watch her and there was no lack of horses in the stable. There were some forty to choose from and the three chose well and rode whole days across the endless plain. There were driving picnics also and Casimir noticed that Manya's delicate wrists handled the reins of the second wagonette with skill. Casimir had sprained his left thumb so that the coachman had to drive his mother and the babies in the first wagonette.

Among the endless "geese" whom Casimir had

hitherto met, none had the talk and mystery of this strange girl. When he returned to Warsaw for the autumn, he longed for Christmas.

"It ought always to be winter, Mademoiselle," he said. And to Manya's unsuspecting "No! Why?" he laughed. "Aren't we told to worship beauty and is there anything lovelier than a girl with perfect ankles skating gracefully? And then there are the dances! You who dance so well, don't you love them and the long sledge drives under winter stars?"

Yes, Manya had returned to loving dancing, but still she preferred the summer—the summer holidays.

"The holidays? When I am here?"

Casimir had long guessed her answer. He said that he would go to his father at once. People did not generally marry governesses, but Manya was different, so entirely different. Everyone in his home loved her; his father chose her for his walking companion; his mother introduced her to all her friends; his sister adored her. They had often invited her father, her brother and her sister to stay in the home; they showered presents and flowers on her on her birthday; they were surely just waiting to welcome her with delight as a new daughter.

But about that, Casimir was mistaken. When he told his parents that he wanted to marry Manya, his father was furious and his mother nearly fainted. Should their eldest son, he on whom all their hopes were fixed, who could bring home as bride the richest, noblest girl of all the country, should he marry a penniless governess? Marry a woman who earned her living by selling her work in other people's houses!

"Casimir, you're mad! People don't marry governesses!"

"People don't marry governesses! What a good thing!" hummed the old Earth as it whizzed round the Sun bringing Summer after Winter and Marie Curie for all of us instead of Madame Manya Casimir Z—.

But Manya who could not foresee the future, was very unhappy. Everyone in the house grew cold to her; yet she could not throw up her post and go away, because she had to send Bronia twenty pounds a year. All she could do was to make up her mind that never, never again would she ever love any man. All the to-morrows took on again their resemblance to all the yesterdays. She gave her lessons, scolded Andzia, shook Julek awake, because every book sent him to sleep, taught her ragged school, read chemistry, played chess, danced, walked. Only one thing sometimes introduced a little excitement: the roads were so badly marked that they would disappear entirely under the snow and the sleigh and its occupants would find themselves buried in a snow-filled ditch. On such occasions, laughter would bring back some of the old gay friendliness.

At that time, her letters home grew longer, but she often hadn't a stamp to send them with or the money to buy one. "I haven't heard from

Bronia," she complained, "but perhaps she hasn't a stamp either." Because of her own sadness she was more able to enter into the troubles of her father, her brother and Hela. To her father she wrote: "Don't worry about us; you have done everything a father could do for us; after all, haven't you given us quite nice characters? We'll be able to earn a living all right, you'll see." And to her brother: "Joseph, borrow a hundred roubles and stay in Warsaw. Don't bury yourself in the country and don't be angry if I do give you advice. Remember our agreement to say anything that comes into our heads. Everybody thinks that to practise in the country would be to bury yourself in a hole and have no career. A doctor without a chemist's shop, a hospital or books will just become a dud, however good his resolutions may be. If that happened to you, darling, I should be desperately unhappy, because now that I have lost all hope of ever being anything myself, all my ambition is fixed on you and Bronia. You mustn't bury the gifts that our family undoubtedly possess. They *must* come out in one of us. The more I despair about myself, the more I hope for you." Manya was also feeling great sympathy for Hela, who had been given up by her lover, and great indignation against young men in general: "Truly," she wrote, "one is learning to have a good opinion of people! If they don't want to marry poor girls, they can go to the devil. No one asks them to do it, but why fall in love with them and then upset them?"

It was a bad moment in Manya's life. She said she was afraid she was catching stupidity from her pupils, which is a fear that comes to many teachers. Her great dreams seemed foolish. "The only dream I have now," she wrote, "is to have a corner of my own where I can live with my father. To get a little independence and a home, I would give half my life. If by any possibility I can leave Z—s, which does not seem very likely, I will get a post in a boarding school in Warsaw and earn a little extra by private lessons. That's all I hope for. Life isn't worth bothering so much about." It was, indeed, a bad moment. But a novel called *On the Banks of the Niemen* fortunately reminded her that ideas like that were not the real Manya. "Where have my dreams gone?" she wrote to Bronia. "I wanted to work for the people, and I have scarcely been able to teach a dozen village boys and girls to read. As to awakening in them a thought of what they are and of what they might do in the world! You couldn't dream of such a thing. Life is hard. I am becoming so mean, so common. Then suddenly a book like this novel gives me a shock and I am miserable about it all." At the same time she wrote to her cousin: "I am in a black humour, for our daily company are frightful west winds, seasoned with rain, floods and mud. There's not a thought of frost and my skates hang sadly in the wardrobe. Perhaps you don't know that in our small hole frost and its advantages are as important as a debate between Conservatives and

Liberals in Galicia! Don't think that your tales bore me. On the contrary it is a true delight to hear that there are places on the earth's surface where people move and even think! I feel things violently with a physical violence! Then I shake myself and get back to myself out of a nightmare and tell myself 'Don't be crushed either by people or by events.' But the need of new impressions, of change, of movement seizes me at moments with such force that I want to do something utterly, utterly foolish to put an end to this eternal sameness. Happily I have so much work that this folly doesn't get hold of me often."

Chapter VII

Change

Manya had desired change and she was to get change. She was to travel. She heard of another pupil who lived in Warsaw, but who was on holiday in far away Belgium and Manya was to join her there. Manya became suddenly doubtful whether she liked so much change as that. She would have to travel alone and have five changes of train. She would surely get lost; or thieves might come into her compartment at night while she slept. But none of these things happened. She found herself safely met by her new employers and introduced to an entirely new world—a world of great wealth which she was expected to share and to enjoy. Her pupil's mother was beautiful and charming. For the first time in her life Manya was close to lovely dresses made by Worth's; she was expected to finger and admire

55 E

soft furs and brilliant jewels; she saw people who were becoming her friends looking at her from the walls where their portraits hung painted by the greatest painters. She moved among all the loveliest things that wealth can give and looked on at all the charm of parties and balls, gaiety and music. Moreover these rich people were human and kind. Mrs. F— liked her, took her everywhere, called her to her friends "The exquisite Miss Sklodovska."

We have not heard what Manya thought of it all, because something far more exciting was about to happen to her. On the hall table lay a letter with the Paris post mark addressed to Miss Sklodovska in Bronia's handwriting—a letter written on squared exercise book paper, written hurriedly between two lectures. What news! Bronia was going to be married! Bronia was inviting Manya to share her home in Paris as soon as she had it! Paris! . . . A University. . . . All her hopes fulfilled?

It was not as simple as that. Manya had known for some time that Bronia was engaged to the cleverest, handsomest, most delightful Polish student in Paris. His name, like that of Manya's own lover, was Casimir, Casimir Dluski. He had been obliged to flee from Poland because he was suspected of having been connected with a plot. In Paris he was watched by request of the Czar's police and had all kinds of odd information entered against him in the books of the Paris Gendarmerie. But, in spite of that, he was a gay

young doctor and he was going to marry Bronia.
So Bronia would never be able to return to Warsaw to take care of her father. That would be
Manya's part, for Hela was not much use for
taking care of anybody.

How lovely, how wonderful, how ideal shone
the future according to Bronia! But Manya wrote
back: "I have been a fool, I am a fool, I shall
always be a fool my whole life through, or rather
to translate into more fashionable language: I
never had any luck! I haven't any luck! I never
shall have any luck!" Thereupon the unlucky
may take heart as they consider what was to
happen to Manya. She went on: "I have dreamed
of Paris as one dreams of salvation, but hope of
getting there fled a long time ago and now that
the possibility of getting there has come to me,
I don't know what to do. I can't talk to father
about it, because I think his heart is set on our
plan of living together next year and I would like
to give him a little happiness in his old age. On
the other hand, my heart breaks when I think
of how my gifts are being wasted and yet gifts
ought to be used." It was that feeling that gifts
ought to be used that made her urge Bronia in the
same letter to put pride in her pocket and beg,
with all her most ingratiating skill, a rich friend
to help Joseph to use *his* gifts. Manya argued that
it would not be only Joseph who would be helped,
but the world which would profit by his skill. All
through her life Manya was to keep the opinion
that one of the noblest works is to help the greatly

gifted to use their gifts for the world. She ended her letter: "My heart is so black, so sad that I feel how wrong I am to talk to you of all this and poison your happiness."

So Manya went home to live for at least a year with her father in a little home of their own. To some people it would have seemed dull, but Manya had a brain and found more sensible talk in her father's house than in any other. She also returned to the strange "winged" secret society and talked and studied.

But Chance had a trick up her sleeve. No one would have suspected, if he walked in May down the quiet tree-planted avenue of Cracow and smelt the purple lilacs in the grass-grown court of No. 66, that there was anything surprising or world-shaking there. In the court, beside the lilacs, there was a little one-storied building with tiny windows. *Museum of Industry and Agriculture* was written in large letters over its doors. Were old ploughshares or prehistoric spades kept there? Not a bit of it! Russia allowed museums to exist. They are always such properly dead places. But any intelligent person can teach in a museum. Manya's cousin was the Director of this one and, secretly, he taught science in it. He had a laboratory where the students could actually touch apparatus.

For the first time in her life Manya Sklodovska entered a laboratory! And *that* was to make a remarkable difference to the great world. She couldn't go there much, only in the evenings and on Sunday. There was no one to teach her when she got there. She worked all alone trying to reproduce experiments described in text books. Her results were sometimes unexpected, but sometimes a tiny success filled her with hope and sometimes a striking failure filled her with despair. But always, she found discovery, or even trying to discover, a wild delight.

When late at night she got home and rolled into bed, something seized her, something grabbed her mind, something spoke to her in the dark. She couldn't sleep. It was as if another someone in herself was talking to her, hammering at her thoughts, telling her what she must get up and do. Her work had found her and was insisting that she must do it. Those test tubes and retorts of the museum were friends and allies of her father's old physical apparatus which she had once loved. Manya Sklodovska had found herself—that self whose clever hands *must* for ever handle tubes and flames, elements and metals, while her clever brain drew conclusions from what her hands did and looked into the future.

But what should she *do*? Hands and brain said go! Love said stay with her father and brother and sister, with her lover Casimir Z—, who was still trying to win his parents' consent to his marriage. Manya met him in the holidays. They walked the mountains together, he told her in long talks of his difficulties and asked her advice.

"If you can't find a way out yourself," exclaimed Manya, at the end of her patience, "don't ask me." She at least knew her own mind at last. She wrote hurriedly to Bronia: "Give me a definite answer. I won't be any trouble to you. You can put me to sleep anywhere. But, I implore you, answer frankly.

Bronia answered frankly; she would have telegraphed if telegrams had not been too dear. Manya would have caught the next train if she had not had so many arrangements to make. She put all her savings on the table and counted them with her father. He added what he could to them. There, before their eyes, lay the round roubles that made Paris possible, only just possible.

Manya could not afford to travel third all the way. In Poland and France third was the cheapest, but Germany had a fourth. It did not matter that the fourth was like a succession of luggage vans. They had no separate compartments and they were bare, except for a bench round the four sides, and thoughtful people took their own stools and sat in the middle. Manya would do that. She would have to take a lot of luggage to save buying in France, but the bulkiest she could send in advance by luggage train—her own mattress, her blankets, her sheets, her table napkins. The only thing she had to buy was a cheap, strong, wooden trunk which she marked proudly M.S. Into it she put her strong, durable clothes, her shoes, her two hats. Then she did up the packages she would take with her in the truck for the journey: food and drink for three days in the train, the stool, her books, a bag of caramels and a rug.

Manya was off to Paris. She was twenty-four and her eyes literally shone with eagerness and joy. The long-hoped-for adventure had begun.

CHAPTER VIII

"I take the Sun and throw it . . ."

"I TAKE the Sun and throw it. . . ." Manya laughed with joy at the words. Where was she? In the heart of Paris where joyous, free things happened, where in lightness of heart her great teacher, Paul Appell, could teach what he pleased, how he pleased; and, if he taught truth, crowds would flock to his teaching.

Manya had arrived early for the lecture and chosen a front seat in the great amphitheatre of the Sorbonne. She put her notebooks and her penholder neatly on the desk in front of her. All around her was the noise of the crowd getting into their places, but Manya did not hear them; she was absorbed in thought. Suddenly there was silence, for the master had come in and, as all his students were ardent mathematicians, they expected a treat.

Appell, with his square head, in his dark severe gown, explained so clearly that the very stars seemed to move obediently into their places as he spoke and the earth seemed at his mercy. He adventured boldly into the furthest regions of space, he juggled with figures and with stars. He said perfectly naturally and fitting the action to the word: "I take the Sun and throw it. . . ."

Manya was happy. How could anyone find

science dull? She thought how exquisite were the
unchanging laws of the universe and how still
more wonderful it was that the human mind
could understand them. Was not Science stranger
than a fairy tale, more delicious than a book of
adventure? It was worth years of suffering she
felt just to hear that phrase uttered by a savant:
"I take the Sun and throw it. . . ."

But how much else Manya had found in Paris!
When she had first jumped from the train in the
smoky, noisy North Station, she had thrown back
her shoulders and breathed deep, not noticing the
smoke. For the first time she was breathing the air
of a free land. Outside the station everything
seemed to her a miracle. The children in the
gutter teased one another in the tongue they
wanted to speak; what a miracle for the Polish
girl who had had to speak Russian! The book
shops sold the books they wanted to sell, the books
of all the world; what a miracle!

But most miraculous of all, that road where she
jumped on her first omnibus and scrambled to the
cheap seats on top, was taking her, Manya Sklodovska, to a university that opened its doors to
women! And what a university! The Sorbonne
was the most famous university in the world.
Even Luther, the German, had confessed that
Paris had the most famous school in the whole
world. The university was being rebuilt; workmen were everywhere; dust and noise were everywhere; classes moved from room to room as the
workmen took possession. But that mattered

nothing to Manya. At last she could learn what she wanted.

From that time on, she began to write her Christian name in French—Marie. With her surname she could do nothing. Her young associates found it too difficult to pronounce and a little on account of it left her alone. In the long corridors they turned to glance back at the simply, poorly-dressed stranger with the airy, fairy hair and intense eyes. "Who is she?" asked one. "A foreigner with an impossible name," answered another. "They say she is always among the first in Physics, but she doesn't talk."

Marie had to work very hard. She had had no idea how ignorant she would find herself in comparison with her companions. Her French turned out not to be as useful as she had expected. She missed whole phrases in a lecture. She found great chasms in her mathematics and physics. She set to work to correct all her defects.

It was well for her that in those first ys she lived with Bronia and Casimir. Bro a was a genius for making things comfortable. She had taken a flat outside Paris where flats were cheaper and had furnished it with borrowed money. She was not the sort of person who lived just anyhow for fear of the risk of not being able to pay back. She had to have pretty things in her home, nicely draped curtains, graceful furniture, a piano and a few bright flowers in a vase. In her little kitchen she cooked exquisitely well-flavoured dishes and cakes, or made tea with tea sent especially from

Poland, because she felt that there were some things Paris could not produce.

The quarter where she lived was, as in medieval times, almost reserved for butchers, and Doctor Dluski's patients were mostly sick butchers. They interviewed him in the little study which was set apart for his use during certain hours of the day. At other times it was Bronia's consulting room where she saw the butcher's wives about their babies. In the evenings work was strictly set aside and the two doctors tried to entice their newly arrived sister to all the fun of the fair. If there was a little money to spend they took her to a cheap seat at the theatre; if there wasn't, they gathered round their own piano or gave a tea party to their exiled Polish friends, when talk and laughter and teasing went on around the oil lamp and the tea-table set with Bronia's homemade cakes. Manya often withdrew early from those parties to work alone in her room, because she felt she had no time to play.

"Come out, Miss Bookworm!" called Casimir one evening; "it is Poland that calls; you have got to come this time. Hat and coat, quick! I've got complimentary tickets for a concert."

"But . . ."

"But me no buts! It's that young Pole we were talking of and very few people have taken seats. We must go to fill the hall. I've got some volunteers and we are going to clap our hands off to give him the feeling of success. If you only knew how beautifully he plays!"

Marie could not resist her gay brother-in-law with his dark, sparkling eyes. Downstairs she hastened, dressing as she went, and ran to catch the old horse bus. She sat in the half-empty hall and watched the tall, thin man with the wonderful face and shock of copper-red hair walk up the platform and open the piano. She listened . . . Liszt, Schumann, Chopin lived again under his marvellous fingers. Marie was passionately moved. The pianist in his threadbare coat, playing to empty benches, did not seem to her an obscure beginner, but a king, almost a god.

The Dluskis asked him to their home. He went, taking with him his beautiful future wife whom Manya's mother had known. Mrs. Sklodovska used to say of the girl that she could never take her out because she was too beautiful. Sometimes the fiery-haired young man would go to the Dluski's piano, and at his touch, the common thing became sublime with heavenly music; for he who played was Paderewski, someday to be world famous, first as a pianist and then as President of a free Poland.

But those days were still far away. In 1891 Marie lived in Paris among a group of Polish exiles who seemed to make a little Polish island in the French city. They were young; they were gay; they were poor. On the fête days of the year, they met for parties in which everything was as Polish as they could make it. They ate Polish cakes, they acted Polish plays, they printed their programmes in Polish and decorated them with

Polish scenes: a cottage in an expanse of snow, a dreamy boy bending over books, a Father Christmas throwing scientific textbooks down a chimney, an empty purse that rats had gnawed. When they acted plays, Marie was too busy to learn a part; but in a tableau, she once represented "Poland breaking her chains." Dressed in a long tunic such as the ancients wore, the colours of the Polish flag draped round her and her fair hair framing her Slav face, she was greeted by all the young people as a very vision of Poland.

Yet to show love for Poland, even in free Paris, was a dangerous thing. Mr. Sklodovski begged Manya not to be seen again in a Polish festivity which could get into the newspapers. "You know," he wrote, "that there are people in Paris noting the names of those who take any part in Polish affairs and this might be a trouble to you and prevent you getting a post later on in Poland. It is wiser to keep out of the limelight."

Marie scarcely needed that hint from her father. She wanted to give all her time to work, to live alone, free from the interruption of the piano, of her brother-in-law's evening chatter, of friends dropping in. And she wanted to live nearer to the university to save her bus fares and the time the bus took.

Sadly, accompanied by both the Dluskis, she left the comfort and friendliness of her sister's home and set out to find her own work place, her own utter solitude.

She was going to live the life of her dreams, a

life entirely given up to study. She would have to do it on one pound a week or rather less. Out of that she would have to pay for her room, her food, her clothes, her paper, her books and her university fees. Could it be done? That was her mathematical problem and, fortunately, she was good at mathematics, but that particular problem would take some doing. "Ah!" she thought, "I needn't eat much!" She had never had time to learn to cook. Her friends said that she didn't even know what went into soup. She didn't know and she hadn't time. She would never dream of taking time from physics to prepare a dinner. So she lived on bread and butter, cherries and tea, with an occasional egg or a piece of chocolate.

Her room was cheap—4s. 6d. a week. It was just an attic under the roof, lit by a sloping window, unheated, with no gas and no water. Her only furniture was a folding iron bedstead with her Polish mattress, a stove, a deal table, a kitchen chair, a washing basin, an oil lamp with a penny shade, a water bucket which she had to fill at the common tap on the landing, a spirit lamp to cook her food, two plates, one knife, a fork, a spoon, a cup, a saucepan, a kettle and three glasses for tea. When visitors came, her trunk was seat enough for two.

Two sacks a year of charcoal, which she bought on the street and carried up, bucket by bucket, all the six storeys, gave her all the warmth she allowed herself. Light she could almost do without. As soon as it began to get dark, she went to the St. Geneviève library and read there, her head in her hands, her elbows on the long table, till closing time at ten at night. After that she only needed oil in her lamp to last her till two in the morning, when she went to bed.

That was food, house, warmth and light settled. As to clothes, Marie could sew and brush and she meant to keep herself neat by brushing and mending, not by buying. She could do her own washing in her basin at the cost of a little soap.

That was a deliciously cheap life she planned in which nothing should interrupt her learning. But girls' bodies have a way of having something to say on their own account. Marie was surprised that often, when she left her books, she turned giddy. She even fainted sometimes on her way to bed before she had time to lie down. When she returned to consciousness, she told herself that she must be ill; but even of that she took no notice, merely thinking she would soon be better.

When her doctor brother-in-law told her she looked ill, she replied that she had been working and turned the conversation with a request for the baby. She had begun to make a great pet of Bronia's new baby and liked to turn attention from herself.

But luckily, one day, Marie fainted in public and the girl who saw it fetched Casimir. By the time he arrived, Marie was well again, but Casimir insisted on examining her. Then without a word he examined the room. Where, he asked, was the food cupboard? Manya hadn't got such a thing. Nowhere was there anything that showed any sign of eating and only a packet of tea to suggest that Marie drank anything.

"What have you eaten to-day?" asked the doctor.

"To-day? ... I don't know ... I lunched ..."

"What did you eat?"

"Cherries. .... Oh, all sorts of things. ..."

In the end Marie had to confess that since yesterday she had eaten a bunch of radishes and half a pound of cherries. She had worked till three in the morning and she had slept only four hours.

The doctor was furious, furious with the little fool, looking at him with innocent, cheerful grey eyes and more furious with himself for not having seen that his clever sister-in-law was a great silly in some things.

Sternly he ordered her to collect what she would want for a week and to come with him. He was so angry he wouldn't talk. At home, Bronia was sent out to buy beefsteak and Marie was ordered to eat it properly underdone in its red gravy and with its crisp potatoes. In less than a week she was again the healthy girl who had so lately come from Warsaw.

Because she was worried about her examination, she was allowed to go back to her attic on condition that she would feed herself sensibly. But alas, the very next day she was living on the air that blows.

Work! . . . Work! . . . Marie was feeling her own brain growing. Her hands were getting cleverer. Soon Professor Lippman trusted her with a piece of original research and she had won her opportunity to show her skill and the originality of her mind. Any day of six she could be seen, in her coarse science overall, standing before an oak table in the lofty physical laboratory of the Sorbonne watching some delicate piece of apparatus or gazing at the steady boiling of some fascinating substance. Other similar workers were round her, men for the most part, utterly silent, doing a thing that was more absorbing than talk.

But when the experiments had come out, the boys looked at the girl, said a word at the door, pressed round her to make friends. She was growing a little less standoffish. Once the boys' eagerness to walk with her became so eager that her friend Mademoiselle Dydyuska had to shoo them away with her parasol. Marie had no time for friendship. With an iron will, a mad love for perfection and an incredible stubbornness she stuck to her work.

She won her *licence* in Physics in 1893 and in Mathematics in 1894, being top of the list in Physics and second in Mathematics. She was also working for perfection in French, refusing to allow any Polish accent to remain on her tongue; she intended to speak French like the French with only a little rolling of the "r," which, though she did not intend it, only added to her charm.

F

She was not too busy to take note of flowers and springtime in Paris. She never forgot that she was a Polish peasant belonging to the fields. She spent Sunday in the country and talked of the lilacs and fruit trees in bloom and the air which was scented with flowers.

When the scorching days of July came, there was another examination. Marie was nervous. With thirty others shut into an airless room she gazed at the paper whose words danced and glimmered before her eyes. She pulled herself together and wrote. She waited, as so many others have done, with a sinking heart for the day of the result. When it came, she crept to listen to the announcement into a corner of the great amphitheatre where she felt very insignificant in the crowd of students and their parents, for she was sure she had done badly.

The noise of talk and of a moving crowd suddenly became silence. The examiner had entered with his list. Marie had no time to listen. The examiner had already spoken the first name:

Marie Sklodovska.

So the holidays had come and Marie had the joy of taking home to Poland her wonderful result. She had other things to take home—presents! For this time she could spend all the money she had left, yes, everything, every penny. She could buy presents for her father, for Joseph, for Hela, and food for her 2,000 mile journey. It was the unbreakable custom with every Pole to arrive home penniless and laden with presents.

In the long summer, all over Poland, her relations feasted and fêted her. But the question that was eating at her heart was: what should she do about the autumn? Where and how could she raise a pound a week for another year at the university? Once more Mademoiselle Dydyuska turned up with her parasol. Whom she used it against this time, nobody knew, but she persuaded the authorities in Warsaw to grant a scholarship to the girl, who, she told them, would bring glory to their city. The great news came to Marie that she would have the Alexandrowitch bursary of £60. It meant another year's learning. Carefully she saved to make the bursary go as far as possible; carefully, after she was able to earn money for herself, she saved to return the bursary money, so that some other poor student might know the joy she had known. When, years after, the bursary secretary received the returned money he was greatly astonished, for no other student had ever thought of making such a return.

So back to work she went, to that work which was no drudgery, but the great love of her whole passionate being. That was the part of Marie's life she loved best, her hard student days, when, working in poverty and alone, with all the power of her youth, she was most herself. She has been called "the eternal student"—one of those people we meet in all the ancient stories of all the old universities: young, poor, greedy for knowledge, believing themselves gifted for some great purpose and driven to attain that purpose at any cost under high heaven.

Marie, working under her old oil lamp, knew herself one with the great scientists, the helpers of

men. She had little to live on, but she lived greatly, gaily, thoughtlessly, rejoicingly. Truth was her daily fun, spoilt occasionally by a tragedy such as the final falling to pieces of a pair of shoes. To get a new pair would upset her spending for weeks; she would have to be hungrier than ever and colder. One night she was so cold that she took all her clothes out of her trunk and piled them on her bed. But she was still cold and there was nothing else movable to heap on her except the chair. So she dragged that on top and had to keep very still till morning lest her odd, warming scaffolding should fall off.

The water in her water jug might be ice in the mornings, but she loved those days so much that she wrote a verse about them:

Harsh and hard she lived to learn.
 Round her swirled the young who seek
Pleasures easy, pleasures stern.
 She alone, long week by week,
Happy, gay, made great her heart.
 When fleeting time took her away
From lands of knowledge and of art
 To earn her bread on life's gray way,
Oft times her spirit sighed to know
 Again the attic corner strait,
Still scene of silent labour slow,
 So filled with memory of fate.

Chapter IX

Marie's Love Story

Marie was in a fix. It was not her first, and was not going to be her last. She had been given a most interesting piece of scientific work to do and she had nowhere to do it. The Society for the Encouragement of National Industry had asked her to make a thesis on the magnetic properties of different kinds of steel. It was just the work she loved. She had been getting on with it most successfully in Professor Lippmann's laboratory, but there simply wasn't room for all the heavy apparatus she needed. She had to analyse minerals and group examples of metals, and she hadn't any idea where she could get the loan of floor space. She told her trouble to a scientific Polish friend, M. Kowalski, who had come to Paris with his wife, partly on his honeymoon, partly to give scientific lectures.

Kowalski looked at her seriously. He saw that the matter was important, but what could he, a stranger in Paris, do about suggesting a room.

"I have an idea!" he exclaimed after a few moment's hesitation. "I do know a man of some importance who works in Lhomond Street at the School of Physics and Chemistry. He might have a room to lend, or at any rate he could give you some advice about it. Come and have tea to-morrow evening after dinner. I'll ask the young man to come along, too. He is well known; you must have heard his name, Pierre Curie."

As Marie entered the sombre boarding-house room where the Kowalskis lodged she noticed a tall young man standing in the embrasure of the balcony window. He looked very young, which surprised her because she was expecting to meet a man who had already made his mark. There was something original and very striking about the stranger, an ease, a grace, which seemed all the more marked under his loosely-fitting clothes. There was a clear transparency in the look with which he welcomed the girl to whom he was being introduced, which made him seem very honest, very simple, very young. She liked his grave, yet almost childlike, smile. They began at once to talk of science, for was not that why they had been brought together?

He was an unusual kind of man, the son of a doctor, who had realised, while Pierre was very young, that he was not the kind of boy who fits well into a mould that suits other people; Pierre wouldn't do for a public school, so he had a private tutor to himself. He had grown up a home-keeping boy, loving his father and mother's company and that of his only brother. He had taken to loving science, and also to delving into his own mind and writing down his opinions in his diary. "Women," he wrote, when he was very young, "love life just for the mere sake of being alive far more than we men: women of genius are very rare. So when we give all our thoughts to some great work which separates us from the ordinary life around us, we have liter-

ally to fight against woman. The mother wants the love of her son even though, through loving her, he should make of himself an imbecile. A woman who loves would be ready to sacrifice the greatest genius in the world for the sake of the love of an hour."

That was a bitter way to think of girlhood or of womanhood, but Pierre had his excuse. In addition to the fact that his observation was sometimes very true, he had had great grief connected with his first love, and he had made up his mind never to speak of it and never to marry. On that fateful evening when he talked science with Marie in the alcove, he was thirty-five. Inside France he was almost unknown, almost neglected, with that strange heart-breaking neglect with which France has the custom of greeting her greatest men, without all the same making them less great.

Outside France he was famous. A discovery that he and his brother had made which had helped to measure very minute quantities of electricity was used with gratitude by the greatest scientists of other countries. His own discovery of the principle of symmetry in crystals was to become a foundation of modern science. He had already given his name to a new balance and a new physical law. He was the honoured master of men like Lord Kelvin; but for all that he was getting only the wage of a superior workman, three pounds a week.

Still, his poverty was somewhat his own fault. He had been offered a post where money was the chief reward, but he had replied, "No, thank you, nothing is more unhealthy for the spirit than preoccupations of that kind." He had been suggested for government honours, and had begged to be excused and he had decided never to accept any decoration of any kind.

So this science-lover of stern and settled character stood before Marie and talked, his long, sensitive hand resting on the table, his still, clear eyes watching her with that deep, calm, detached inspection of theirs. Perhaps suddenly he remembered that old opinion of his—"Women of genius are rare."

At first, conversation had been, as it would be when four people meet, quite general. Then Pierre and Marie had got on to science. Had she not come purely for scientific business? With a touch of deference, she questioned the great man who looked so young, and listened to his suggestions. Then he talked of himself, a thing he so rarely did, of his own aims and of his crystallography, which was puzzling and interesting him and whose laws he was seeking. A sudden thought darted through his mind: how strange it is to find one's self talking to a woman about the work one loves, employing technical terms and complicated formulas, and finding that woman, though charming and young, grow interested and keen, finding her understand, and finding her discuss details with faultless perception. . . . What a delicious experience! He looked again at Marie, at her lovely hair, at her hands, made rough by chemical acids and housework, at her grace, at her absolute freedom from coquetry—so attractive and disconcerting a thing. That was the girl who had worked for years in Poland with the hope of reaching Paris, and was now there, working alone, penniless, in an attic.

"Are you going to live in Paris always?" he asked.

"No, of course not," replied Marie. "If I manage my examination this summer I shall return to Warsaw. I should like to come back in the autumn, but I don't know if I shall be able to afford it. In the end I shall teach in a Polish school and try to be useful. No Pole may desert her country."

The conversation slipped off to the misery of Poland, to her oppressive masters. Pierre, whose one thought had been scientific discovery, listened surprised and distressed to a tale of human beings struggling to be free. Perhaps he thought of how great losses truth and knowledge may suffer when the scientists are obliged to give their thoughts away from science. Perhaps he began to dream that he must fight Poland and keep this rare genius for scientific Paris. At any rate, he was not going to lose touch with her. He took to meeting her at the Physics Society, where she went to hear about new discoveries. He sent her a copy of the limited edition of his own new book. He saw her from time to time at work in her linen overall among her apparatus in Lippmann's laboratory.

Then Pierre asked for Marie's address and called at 11 Rue des Feuillantines. Perhaps he remembered it as the street in which Pasteur had, also, once lived. As, after six flights of stairs, he entered the attic, the doctor's son was moved by the sight of the extreme poverty of the room. Yet how well it suited Marie! Never had she seemed so lovely as when she came to meet him in her threadbare frock across that almost empty room; so thin, so ascetic, so on fire, so stubborn, so self-willed she looked, so beautifully framed in emptiness.

All Pierre's bitterness went, like fog when the sun breaks through. They talked and he went back to work with quite another spirit; what had seemed to him little worth doing became more important and more clear. His new theory worked itself out into a most brilliant doctor's thesis and he made the discovery that one woman, at any rate, so far from killing genius in a man, had awakened it. He gave himself better to his high thoughts because he had given his heart to Marie.

But what of her heart? Pierre tried to find out. He took her into the lovely French country they both loved; together they gathered marguerites and brought them home to lend an air of whiteness and grace to the attic. He took her home to Sceaux, outside Paris, to meet his mother and his delightful old father. Marie found herself as if in a second home, a home oddly like hers in Warsaw, among calm, affectionate people who loved one another, loved books, loved nature and, above all, loved science. They talked of beautiful Poland, of Marie's long walks through its beautiful wide-spreading meadows, of her joy at the thought of the coming holidays there and among the Swiss mountains.

"But you are coming back in October?" exclaimed Pierre, a sudden chill clutching his heart! "It would be a sin on your part to abandon science."

Marie was not deceived. She knew already that he meant it would be a sin to abandon him.

But Poland held her heart. Yet she said, looking shyly up at him, "I think you are right. I should very much like to come back."

It was not long before Pierre felt brave enough to put his thought into words and to ask her to be his wife. But that she could never be, she said. She could never marry a Frenchman and turn her back on Poland. So many discussions followed that word, for Pierre knew that science was on his side and he could not believe that it was anyone's duty to give up science, which belonged to the whole world, for the sake of working for a mere country.

So Marie went home again for her holidays promising Pierre nothing but that he should always be her friend. He wrote her long persuading letters. He planned to meet her in Switzerland for a few days, but she was meeting her father there and he decided that his presence might spoil the girl's perfect holiday. He told her by post all his thoughts and his hesitations, never forgetting to slip in his opinion that the only dream that a man should live for was the scientific dream. "In politics," said he, "you never know what you may be doing; you may be ruining your country while trying to help her. If you dream of helping humanity, you don't know how to do it. But science is solid. Any discovery, however small, that you make in that, remains made. Truth, once found, can't disappear and can never be wrong.

Believe me,
Your devoted,
Pierre Curie."

Marie liked to write to him about her freedom. "Talk!" he answered. "We're all slaves, slaves of our affections, slaves of prejudice, slaves when we have to earn a living, wheels in a machine. We *have* to yield something to the things around us! If we yield too much, we are poor mean things; if we don't yield enough, we are crushed."

In October Marie returned to Paris, and it wasn't only she who was stubborn. What about that yielding to the things around one, about which Pierre spoke? He began to wonder if it should be he who should yield. The thought had no sooner come than he acted on it! He offered to give up Paris and to go to Poland. For a time he would give up science and teach French for a living; then somehow he would get back into scientific work.

Marie confided her hesitations to Bronia and asked her what she thought about that wonderful offer of Pierre's to give up his country. For herself, she felt that no one had the right to ask such a sacrifice of another. She was overwhelmed at the thought that Pierre had offered it to her. Pierre, too, went to the Dluskis. They were entirely on his side.

Bronia began to go with Marie to visit his parents, and heard from his mother so tender an account of the wonderful son Pierre was, that she knew that her sister's happiness would be safe in his hands.

Ten months more Marie hesitated, and then the two who had both promised themselves that they would never marry abandoned their high-flown ideas, and said yes to happiness.

Marie's brother wrote her a charming letter from Poland full of understanding. It was as if Poland itself spoke to tell the Polish girl that she could do more good to Poland by marrying a French scientist who happened to be Pierre Curie than she could by returning to be a schoolmistress in Warsaw. And, indeed, all that was about to happen showed that Marie had chosen the right.

So Marie could plan her wedding in all happiness, and what an odd wedding it was to be!

On the 26th of July, 1895, the sun rose in a clear sky, and Marie Sklodovska with it. Her beautiful face was lit with joy as she did her lovely hair and put on her new navy-blue dress with the striped blue blouse that Casimir Dluski's mother had given her. She hadn't wanted a real wedding dress; she was glad to have a new one because she only possessed one she wore every day, but she much preferred something useful that she could wear afterwards in the laboratory.

When she was dressed, Pierre fetched her and they left by the bus to catch the train to Sceaux, where the wedding was to be. Down the Boulevard St. Michel the heavy horses clop-clopped, passing the Sorbonne that the two looked at with loving eyes, for had it not brought them together?

At Sceaux there were to be no guests except Bronia and Casimir, Mr. Sklodovski and Hela, who had come all the way from Warsaw. They couldn't afford a gold ring or a wedding breakfast. For wedding presents, the most important were two shining bicycles, given them by a cousin, on which they were going to spend their honeymoon.

Said the one father to the other father, as they met the bride and bridegroom in the garden after the wedding, "You will have in Marie a daughter you can love, for since the day of her birth she has never given me a moment's pain."

CHAPTER X

Madame Curie

PIERRE and Marie set out for an unusual honey-moon. They had no tickets to get and no rooms to reserve, because they were going off on bicycles just wherever their fancy led. They strapped a few clothes to the bicycles and, as the summer had been wet, two long rubber mackintoshes. Their tyres glided silently over the wet roads; bright, fitful sunshine flecked the tall trunks of the trees that make an avenue of all French roads; overhead, the heavy summer leaves dappled the road with shade like a snakeskin and shook rain-drops on the travellers from the last shower.

Upon what an adventure they were setting out, the two alone together! They couldn't see the end of it or imagine how exciting it was going to be, any more than they could see the end of the long avenue or know where they would sleep the night.

Pierre had always loved to wander in lonely woods. He liked them cool and wet, and, when he came out on to the rocky hillsides, he liked the smell of rosemary and marjoram and eglantine that made a wild jungle there. It was all one to him whether he walked by day or by night, by dawn or gloaming; whether he ate at eleven or three, seven or ten. Now all the things he cared for were lovelier still, because Marie was with him and she didn't bother him about time or punctuality.

They were not going to be extravagant; there should be no hotels for them. When they came to a village at evening, they found a simple inn, a place with one large tap-room, with a few tables and many chairs. The "Patron" spread a clean white cloth for them and brought them thick, hot soup. After dinner, they went up the creaking wooden stairs, along a rambling passage to a room where the light of one candle was not likely to show up the faded paper. French village inns are often like that; the supper is good, the bed is clean and delicious, and the charge small.

Next day after breakfast on coffee and rolls, they pedalled on along another highway under the trees with the forest on either hand. A long green ride that led into mysterious depths of trees tempted them; they dismounted and left their bicycles at a roadside cottage; saw that they had their compass safe, because it is easy to be lost in those great French forests; put apples in their pockets and found their feet sinking through soft moss into squelching mud. Lovely! For them, there was no such thing as direction, no such thing as time, and nobody to wonder when they would be back.

Pierre went in front, striding along absent-mindedly. Marie followed with shorter steps, but keeping up all the same. She was hatless, though at that time other women never walked without a hat. It wasn't the only fashion she was to set. Her skirt, which was meant to trail on the ground and plaster her shoes with caked mud, was gathered quite shockingly high into an elastic band, so that her ankles showed! Her shoes were thick and sensible and her leather belt had pockets for a knife, money and a watch. She could hear well enough what Pierre said, covering the ground there in front as if he had a train to catch. He was evidently talking to her, though, as he never turned his head, it might have been the trees he was addressing on the quaint customs of crystals. There is no conversation more learned or more difficult to follow than a conversation on crystals, or to put it more scientifically, on crystallography. Marie listened with joy, and her answers and remarks and suggestions were as clever as Pierre's, so that it seemed as if the two voices were the expression of one thought.

Marie was beginning to grow tired, when suddenly they came to an opening in the forest; and in the opening was a reedy pool. Marie threw herself down on the bank to bask in the sun, and Pierre went hunting like a small boy for what the pool might contain: dragonflies, tritons, salamanders. Far out in the water there were water-lilies; nearer at hand, yellow irises in bloom. He wanted them to decorate Marie, but there was no boat. A little way away a tree had fallen over the water—the very thing, a little slippery, perhaps, but what did a wetting matter to a lover? Luck was with him, however, and he was soon back arranging a crown of rather damp lilies and irises in his wife's hair.

Then, as if he had suddenly seen something to hunt, he crept on all-fours quietly close to the water again. Marie was not attending; it was so delicious to sit and do nothing in the August heat. Suddenly she screamed and looked with horror at her hand. A cold, wet frog was sitting in it!

"Don't you like frogs?" asked Pierre surprised; he had always liked them himself.

"Yes, but not in my hand."

"What a mistake! They are such jolly things to watch. Look at him; isn't he handsome?"

But he relieved her of the handsome clamminess and let it go back to its pool to the joy of two of the party.

So they went on with the walk and the talk, Marie wearing her startling crown, till they reached the road again and their bicycles.

In mid-August, having gone round Paris by far woodland ways, they came to Chantilly in the north, a town buried in immense forests, where nowadays racehorses always peep at passers-by from their lordly stables. Marie and Pierre were due to join the family at a farm in the woods called "La Biche," or The Hind. There they found Bronia, Casimir and baby Hélène, whom everyone called Lou; Grannie Dluska, Professor Sklodovski and Hela.

A farm in those woods has a charm of its own; never a sound comes near except the barking of a dog, the snapping of a branch, a woodman's distant axe against a tree-trunk, a hasty flutter of a startled pheasant or the skurry of a hare. Everywhere, as far as a man can walk or an eye can see, is an invitation to come in May, for the earth is hidden under the yellow, withering leaves of lilies-of-the-valley.

Inside the farm they talked apace, and often with Lou, who was beautiful, comic and gay and three years old. Sometimes they talked of solemn science with Professor Sklodovski and sometimes of the mysteries of bringing up children. Sometimes they discussed medicine and politics with Pierre's father and mother, who came from Sceaux on visits. France is the land for great talk, and often Marie was surprised to hear with what terrible vigour her French father-in-law and his friends talked politics. Politics were their very life; they cared intensely how their country was governed, and in free France they could say what they liked, which made their talk interesting. But Pierre was different. He disliked politics, because he said he was not clever at getting angry. But when a policy was unjust or cruel, he took sides—the side of the oppressed and persecuted.

So the honeymoon came to an end and Pierre and Marie settled to housekeeping in a Paris flat, and a strange, uncommon housekeeping it was! There were to be no visitors, so there were only two chairs. If a mistaken stranger toiled up the four storeys to pay a formal call and found the couple at home working, he had only to look round for a seat to see, without being told, that there was no place for him. The most pushing would beat a retreat in humbler mood. The Curies did not intend to have time to entertain. Marie, at any rate, would have, as it was, to do the work of two women: the work of a wife, which most wives find enough, and that of a scientist, which most scientists find more than enough.

She determined to make her home as simple and as little time-wasting as possible. There were to be no rugs to shake, no armchair or sofa to brush, nothing on the walls to dust, nothing to polish. The table, the two chairs and the bookshelf were of unpolished deal, which is a pleasant, untroublesome wood. The room depended on simplicity and a vase of fresh flowers for its beauty, while books, a lamp and piles of papers on physics showed it to be a scholar's den. Two people who loved one another, who loved Nature and learning, could desire nothing more. Yet they had to be fed. Doubtless that seemed a pity to them both, but Marie would not again neglect facts.

The first thing she bought to help her with her housekeeping was a black notebook with *Accounts* printed in letters of gold on the cover. She knew that faultless household arithmetic was a most important foundation of a happy home, especially of a home that had to be run on £240 a year exactly.

Her cooking would have to be faultless, too, or Pierre's digestion would go wrong. In addition, she had to find some scheme by which the dinner would cook itself while she spent most of the day at the laboratory doing science. Facts are fierce, strong things, but brains can use them against themselves. The first point was to make the day long. She got up early to go to market; she came home to make the bed and sweep the floor and prepare the evening dinner. Oh, that cooking! She had taken cooking lessons from Bronia and Madame Dluska before her marriage, but one doesn't learn much from lessons; mistakes are far better teachers. It was all very well that Pierre didn't know what he ate, and was as pleased when the dinner was wrong as when it was right, but Marie couldn't bear the idea that her French mother-in-law, a member of that famous cooking nation, might think that Polish girls couldn't cook. She read over and over again her book of recipes, she learned them as if they were science; she wrote notes in the margin and kept a record of her successes and failures. But there are things that printed recipes forget to tell you. Does one put beef to boil in hot or cold water? How long do beans take to boil? What keeps a stick of macaroni from sticking fast to the next piece? Those were mysteries needing a scientific experiment. Little by little, Marie grew clever; she invented dishes that could be left on the gas to cook while she was out; she calculated exactly the height of the gas flame that this or that stew would need for such and such hours; and, having set her burner exactly, she left the house and spent eight hours at the laboratory. Let no one say that a knowledge of science is no use for cooking.

When she walked home with Pierre in the evening, she bought the groceries or the fruit. Then at home, dinner over, her household work finished and expenditure entered in the notebook, she took out her books to study for another degree, and went on with it till two in the morning. It was a long day that stretched from 6.0 a.m. to 2.0 a.m. But still she was able to write to her brother: "All is well with us—health good and life kind. I am getting the flat gradually as I want it, but I intend that it shall be so simple it won't give us any worries or need any looking-after, because I have very little help. A woman comes for an hour a day to wash-up and do the hardest part of the work."

They had no excitements. They went frequently to see Pierre's parents at Sceaux, but they took their work with them and had two rooms set apart for them so that they might be just as if they were at home, just as hard-working. They scarcely ever went to the theatre and they went to nothing else. They could not even afford to go to Hela's wedding in Warsaw. They worked the year round with only a few days' holiday at Easter, till it was August again and Marie's examination in full swing.

Again she passed first on the list. Pierre threw an arm proudly round her neck and marched her home. No sooner had they arrived there than they pumped their bicycles, filled their bags, and set off for the mountains of Auvergne.

Marie wrote of that holiday: "What a radiant memory we have of a certain sunny day, when after a long, painful climb, we found ourselves crossing a fresh green Aubracian meadow in the clear air of those high tablelands. Another vivid memory is of an evening when we were caught by twilight in the gorge of the Truyère, and up the valley came, as by enchantment, a far-away melody from a boat disappearing down the stream. We had miscalculated our distances and couldn't get back to our beds before dawn. Then we met a string of carts whose horses took fright at our bicycles and obliged us to cut across ploughed fields. When we got back to the road the high tableland was bathed in the moon's unreal light and the cows, in the paddock for the night, came gravely across one by one to gaze at us with their big, calm eyes."

After holiday came work again, and life went on teaching Marie Curie as it had taught Manya Sklodovski, with great blows of hardship, that the best things in the world have to be paid for dearly.

Marie wanted a baby as much as she wanted Science, and as much as she wanted to be able to share everything with Pierre. But she found that this time she just couldn't do everything. She could not stand eight hours studying the magnetization of steel, and she could not bicycle all day with Pierre among the blue bays of Brittany. She was surprised and disgusted to find that she had to yield to some things. When her father came from Poland on purpose to give her an early holiday, Pierre wrote her charming letters in simple Polish, because he was finding the language difficult, but was proud of his progress.

"My little girl, so dear, so sweet, whom I love so much. I got your letter to-day and I am very happy. Here, there is nothing new, except that I miss you; my very soul has fled with you." And Marie answered, making her Polish easy for him: "It is fine. The sun is shining. It is hot. I am very sad without you. Come quickly. I sit watching from morn till eve and still you do not come. I am well. I work as much as I can, but Poincaré's book is harder than I expected. I must talk to you about it and we must go over together what I have found so hard."

Then Irène came to add to Marie's work and joy. She called her her little queen; fed her herself; washed and dressed her, and would have done without a nurse had not the doctor ordered her to have one.

So now Marie had four things to take all her time instead of three: the laboratory, her husband, her house and her daughter. When she wanted to work, Irène was cutting her teeth and crying the house down; or Irène had a cold, or she had knocked her head, or she was a little feverish. Then both the great scientists, who happened to be her father and mother, had to sit up all night to watch a blue-eyed scrap. Sometimes, even when Irène was quite well, Marie, busy with science at the laboratory, would be seized with panic, leave her reports and rush off to the park to see if Nurse had mislaid her baby. No! There was Nurse pushing the pram with Irène safely inside. When Nurse left, Irène found a devoted slave in her grandfather, with whom Marie could leave her whenever the laboratory was having its turn.

But no one can wonder that Irène's mother grew thin. She was lucky, however, and thinness made her more beautiful than ever, with a sort of noble, ghostly beauty. She was almost unreal, as if the wind might have blown her away, except for her great brow and intense dreamy eyes.

CHAPTER XI

The Great Discovery

MARIE had been working at the laboratory like any other distinguished student of science. She had a double master's degree and a fellowship and had written a thesis on the magnetization of tempered steel. Still in front of her was the title that the most ambitious of the learned coveted—that of Doctor. To win that, it was necessary to discover something unknown before, to solve an unsolved problem. There were many unsolved problems, some of them might have no solution. A man might work a whole lifetime and at the end find that his time and his life had been thrown away. Nature, as Shakespeare says, has a great gift of "taciturnity." What, among all things unknown, did Marie choose to try to know?

Pierre was the Head of her laboratory. He was the person whose advice she would take and, moreover, he was a physicist of great knowledge and experience. He would surely be able to suggest something which it was necessary to know, something which would help mankind when known and also lead on to further knowledge. Was there any dark ignorance which blocked some entrancing pathway of the route to knowledge? The two often discussed the question. But one day, turning over the pages of a scientific journal where the latest discoveries were discussed, Marie stopped short at the account of the work of a certain Henri Becquerel which had interested her and Pierre when it first appeared a year before. She read it again. She re-read it with care.

Things which have light in themselves! Things which have never caught light from the sun or even from the stars but which have light in themselves! Interesting? Marie was very interested.

Röntgen had then recently discovered new rays called X-rays and doctors had used them to look through human skin and see the things it hid. Then Poincaré had wondered if there might not be other rays, perhaps somewhat like X-rays.

which certain light-carrying bodies give off under the action of light. That question had interested Becquerel and he had studied certain substances to see if he could find those rays, supposing they existed. In studying a rare metal called Uranium, he had come upon something most surprising and most new: the salts of Uranium gave off rays without any contact with light at all; they were spontaneously light giving. No one had ever met such a thing before; no one could understand the strangeness of that light or explain it. Becquerel knew certain things about it: for instance, that a Uranium compound placed on a photographic plate surrounded by black paper, repeated the photograph through the paper and also used the surrounding air to discharge an electroscope. Surprising rays indeed!

Becquerel had discovered the fact that this strange radiation existed in the world. Marie determined to explain it. That should be the subject of her Doctor's thesis. The thing might be as small as it would, but it should not escape her. She would find out what that radiation came from, what was its origin and its cause, what, in fact, was its nature, or simply what it was. To find out what a thing is, is to explain it.

There were no books to refer to, except Becquerel's paper which had not gone far into the problem. Nobody in the world knew anything about her subject, so she could have no teacher. She was in for a wild adventure into an unknown world.

But just as an explorer, who plans to penetrate into the secrecy of the Brazilian forest, needs a ship to take him to the Amazon, so Marie needed a room in which her experiments could begin. It was not easy to find. Pierre enquired among his friends. But no one could think of anywhere suitable that was not used for something more important. Perhaps, suggested the Director of the School of Physics, the old storeroom on the ground floor would do. It was the home of spiders and their webs and cluttered up with machines and stores, but there was floor space.

In that odd corner, Marie installed herself. She was fortunately well accustomed to discomfort. In the winter she had to content herself with 11 degrees above freezing point. It didn't matter for her, but her instruments were more delicate and were apt to go wrong when they had to put up with hardships. *They* made difficulties when damp poured out of the walls and *they* needed an even temperature. Electrometers are highly sensitive things. Marie had to take their humours into consideration and make allowances for them.

So she began with her Uranium rays. What she had to do was to measure a certain capacity of theirs. She had to find out just how able they were to force the air to carry electricity and just how long it took them to discharge the charge of an electroscope.

Her electroscope was a metal case with two holes in its side. In it a vertical brass strip B was attached to a block of sulphur SS inside the lid—

a good insulator. Joined to the strip B was a horizontal wire, ending at one end in a knob C and at the other in a condenser plate P^1. Also attached

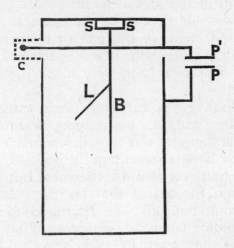

to the strip B was a strip of gold leaf L. The metal case was connected to earth. A charge of electricity was given to the electroscope and then a substance to be tested was placed on a condenser plate P attached to the outer case. That substance would give conductivity to the air between plates P and P^1 and the charge of the electroscope would begin to leak away. As it leaked, the gold leaf L would fall gradually.

Marie watched what was happening through a miscroscope and a hole in the case. The time taken by the gold leaf to fall was in proportion to the strength of the Uranium rays.[1] In a few

[1] From the *Encyclopaedia Britannica*.   H

weeks, she had become quite sure that the radio-activity of her Uranium—the power of the rays —was in proportion to the *quantity* of pure Uranium in the specimens she placed on P and that it was not affected by the chemical make-up of the specimens or by light or temperature or anything outside itself. It was, so to speak, a very independent character, very much itself. What was it?

She could get no further in her investigation of this strange radiance by studying Uranium. Perhaps, she thought, this tiny, independent original character lives in something else besides Uranium? No one had ever found it elsewhere, but that was no reason for saying that no one ever would. Marie could but look. She determined to examine *every known chemical substance*. What a determination that was! Every known . . . !

And, in addition to every known chemical substance, there was a husband to be looked after and a house, and Irène to be dressed and fed and played with and taught. But Marie Curie knew all about work. A guess had floated into her mind, a guess that might have floated into anybody's mind, but hadn't, the guess that if Uranium gave light of itself, surely, in the great universe, there were other substances that did the same thing.

Yes, there were. Marie found another called Thorium. It was then that she gave the name *radio-activity* to this spontaneous giving out of light.

So she had gone through all the chemical substances known, those substances which, combined in myriads of different ways and proportions, make up the whole world. Two of them were radio-active; but why? What, indeed, was the explanation of their strange and beautiful power? She seemed no nearer to the explanation she sought, and what else was there to do when she had been through all known chemical substances?

Well, there were all the things in the world, the finished articles. Marie had a delicious gift of curiosity. She decided to go to the museum and start on the minerals. Those that contained Uranium or Thorium would be radio-active, of course, and those that had neither of the two would be inactive. Other people had recorded what the minerals were made of; Marie had only to take their records and begin with those that were suspect, with those, that is, which were related to the minerals containing Uranium or Thorium.

When she found an active mineral, she measured the amount of Uranium in it and the same for Thorium and then the radio-activity of the whole. One and one should have made two, but they made eight!

$$1+1=8\ !\ !\ !$$

The radio-activity of the mineral she was examining was much stronger than the radio-activity of the Uranium and Thorium in it. Yet she knew by experiment that that was impossible. She had to do her experiments over again, because there must have been a mistake.

If there had been a mistake, she had made it again, because the result was the same. Over and over . . . and over . . . and over again, twenty times over, she did her experiment; but the result was always the same.

There could be but one explanation: the minerals must contain, in very small, unperceived quantity, a quite unknown substance which was very much more radio-active than either Uranium or Thorium.

So, in 1898, something existed which was absolutely unknown to man. Marie said to Bronia: "This ray, which I can't explain, comes from an unknown element . . . it is there; it has only to be found! We are sure of its existence, Pierre and I, but the Physicists, to whom we have spoken of it, think we have made a mistake in our experiments and advise us to be more prudent. But I am convinced that I am not mistaken."

Marie was deeply excited; for what might not that unknown element turn out to be? She had written once: "Life is not easy for any of us— what does that matter? We must persevere and have confidence in ourselves. We must believe that our gifts are given to us for some purpose and we must attain to that purpose whatever price we may have to pay for it."

On April 12th, 1898, Marie Curie published the formal statement: "Pitchblende and Chalcolite are much more radio-active than Uranium itself. This fact is very remarkable and leads us to believe that these minerals may contain an element which is much more active than Uranium . . ."

She *believed* in the new element, but she had to see it, to be able to show it to men's eyes. Pierre Curie, who up to that moment had been keenly interested in his wife's work and had constantly discussed it with her, gave up his own work and turned to labour side by side with her in the effort to bring to the light of day that hidden, secret element. Two minds and four hands were thenceforth going to fight the tiny thing. Marie had discovered that there must be the element. That was her share. After that she and Pierre shared equally in all the work to be done.

They chose a pitchblende to study because it was four times more active than the Uranium which it contained. Yet all the elements of pitchblende were well known to all scientists. The unknown must, they argued, be *very* small to have escaped the notice of careful scientists. It might be a hundredth part of pitchblende, they suggested. What would they have thought at the outset of their work if they had guessed that it was only a millionth part?

They began to break up pitchblende into its elements and to measure the radio-activity of each separate element. As they worked, it became evident that radio-activity dwelt in two chemical fractions of pitchblende; there were two unknown substances. In July, 1898, they found one of the two.

"You must name it," said Pierre to Marie.

Thoughts flashed through her mind. The discovery would be famous, it would be written about in all countries, therefore she would call it after her oppressed country, Poland. The fierce oppressors should know that Poland could give gifts to the world. She whispered to Pierre the substance's name: "Polonium."

Then she went home to make fruit jelly, to wash and dress Irène, to write down the baby's weight in a diary and to record that she was cutting her milk teeth, that she could also make a sign with her hand to mean "thank you" and that she could say "gogli, gogli, go!"

But the time for holidays had come. Polonium and the unknown—that *other* one—were left in the damp laboratory and the baby, the bicycles and the scientists took train for the high hills of Auvergne. Among the little towns with their great cathedrals, their strange, spiked hills crowned with ancient chapels, their extinct volcanoes, two people walked and talked of that *other*, that something which no man or woman had seen. They looked from Clermont to the flat hill where the first French hero, Vercingetorix, had taught invincible Caesar the bitter taste of defeat. They walked in the town where Bertrand du Guesclin lay buried, he who had first made France feel she was a nation. They watched from the heights one of the most ancient roads go by, the "tin road" along which the Phoenicians had carried tin from uncivilized Britain to the cultured East. All past history seemed alive around them and in their minds, like a little restless star, twinkled the thoughts of that unknown and future thing whose power is still a mystery for us all.

In the autumn, the three Curies returned to work: Irène to produce more teeth and to learn to walk on two feet instead of four paws; and her father and mother to seek the stranger in the damp laboratory.

On December the 26th, 1898, in a paper for the Academy of Science, they announced quite quietly: "The new radio-active substance contains a new element to which we propose to give the name Radium . . . the radio-activity of Radium must be enormous."

Chapter XII

A Light in the Dark

So the mysterious and radiant stranger had a name, but no one had yet seen its face, not even Pierre and Marie who had given it its name of Radium. It had not, like all respectable and real substances, been touched, seen, put in a bottle, or even weighed. That question of weighing was very important. Weight—"atomic weight"—was to a scientist the very proof of existence. Something existing in the mind of Pierre and Marie, whose atomic weight even they did not know, was not scientifically there at all in the opinion of the scientists. No, Pierre and Marie had to get hold of Radium and weigh it. When they had done that, scientists would believe in it.

"It is in pitchblende," thought the Curies, "and it is too small to be seen; but perhaps if we could get hold of an enormous quantity of pitchblende and extract all the Radium from it, we should have a piece large enough to see."

But how were they to get hold of a really enormous quantity of pitchblende, say a hundred tons? And where could they put it if they had it? And how could they work on it even if they could house it?

The scientist takes one step at a time. First let them get hold of the pitchblende. They knew where great quantities were to be found, because the Bohemians used it in the manufacture of their beautiful glass; but it was expensive and the Curies had no money worth talking about. But the Bohemians did not, of course, make glass of pitchblende itself; they extracted Uranium from it for the manufacture of glass and threw out the useless dust in mighty powdery heaps in the forest of St. Joachimsthal. "Radium and Polonium," said the Curies, "are not in Uranium; so they must be in that waste dust. Perhaps the manufacturers could be persuaded to sell their waste dust cheap."

"Sell?" said the manufacturers kindly. "We'll give it to you if you will pay for taking it away." Even that transport was expensive enough, but the Curies poured out their savings and sent them to Bohemia.

That was settled. The dust would be arriving, whole railway trucks of it. Where in the world would they put it?

Pierre and Marie went round to the great home of Science, the Sorbonne. Surely in that vast set of buildings, some unwanted room could be found for their valuable and exciting dust; but no! They had to go back to their own school of physics and even there nothing satisfactory could be spared them. The only place available was a shed on the other side of the courtyard from their laboratory. And what a shed! The glass roof was broken and the rain would rain through and upset any experiment that had to be kept dry. There was no floor, only a badly tarred surface; there was no furniture, except an old kitchen table or two, a blackboard and an old stove with a rusty iron chimney. In summer the workers would be cooked, because the roof was of glass. In winter, they would freeze when the outside world froze, because the stove gave no heat; or they would be soaked if it happened to rain. Not that that mattered much, for the room was not fitted with a fume cupboard to carry away the poisonous fumes, so that most of their work would have to be done out of doors. Still "Beggars can't be choosers," says an old adage, so the Curies settled down to making the shed do.

The great morning came. The heavy cart horses with their bells and pointed black fur collars, brought their big coal cart to rest outside the school of physics. Perhaps they looked round surprised at the eager pair who rushed out hatless, in science overalls, with exclamations of joy to welcome their load. Not so was coal generally received.

But the load was not coal; it was sacks of brown dust. Marie could not wait for the sacks to be carried in; excitedly, in the street under the horses' solemn eyes, she seized the string with which one was tied and began to tear it undone. This was pitchblende! Her pitchblende! Or rather the part of pitchblende that mattered. Curiosity was in her heart, her eyes, her tingling, working fingers. At last, she was able to plunge both hands into the brown, dull-coloured dust and pine-needles from the Bohemian pine forest. Was Radium, the radiant stranger, really in that? Would she find stars in the dust? Marie was going to get it out, even if she had to boil down mountains of that dingy dust.

The first ton of sacks was carried into the shed and the work began, four years' work, the best and happiest and hardest years of Marie's life.

In a great iron cauldron, she boiled down the dust, stirring it perpetually with an iron rod nearly as tall as herself. She stuck to her work all day long, even eating at the shed so as not to interrupt her task. She might have been seen any day, her hair blowing in the wind, her dusty overall flecked and tattered with acids, stirring her ill-tempered mud. She had chosen the man's work of hard manual labour out of doors, while Pierre sat at the table indoors trying to discover the properties of Radium by means of delicate, precise experiments. Sometimes she worked more than forty pounds of dust at a time, filling the shed with great pots of precipitates and liquids. She carried heavy weights, lifted pots to pour their contents into others and stirred and stirred the boiling cauldron.

After an entire day spent at the shed, with such hard work as that, Marie had her nursery work at home. She washed Irène and put her to bed and hoped to be able to go and sit in the study with Pierre. But Irène thought differently. No sooner was Marie's back turned, than a little piteous "Mé" came from the nursery . . . "Mé!"

So back went Marie to sit with her baby till she slept. Pierre was not pleased about that; he wanted Marie's time too. But when Irène was asleep husband and wife sat together studying far into the night.

When to-morrow came, they worked again. Where was that Radium? Would they never see it? The days lengthened into months; the months were more than twelve and the second year was slipping into the third, and the third into the fourth. They worked as in a dream, thinking only of one thing, talking only of one thing. "What will it be like when we do see it?" asked Marie one day when she was taking a little time off to pace up and down the courtyard with Pierre.

"I hope it will be a beautiful colour," said Pierre.

In 1900, a French chemist, André Debierne, came to help them and discovered, before ever they had caught a glimpse of Radium or Polonium, a "brother" element which he called Actinium.

Time after time, the heavy horses brought more tons of pitchblende waste to the gate. Every day with her *terrible* patience, Marie was extracting from it a substance in which Radium was more and more concentrated. But still it hid, still it kept itself to itself and preserved its secret.

She had terrible patience, but difficulties were crowding in on the two. She and Pierre had not enough money to live and they had not enough time to work. Pierre had to do a great deal of teaching to earn the £240 on which they lived and that took time from Radium and still was not enough to pay their expenses and those of Irène's nurse. So Pierre tried to get a university post where his work would be more advanced and better paid; where, perhaps, he would have a real laboratory, equipped with electricity for his experiments and where he would not have so many lessons a day and so many wearying corrections at night.

But, unfortunately, posts are not always given to those who do the best work; they often go to the friends of the principal or to those who know the art of praising themselves. When an opportunity came to apply for such a post, Pierre was told that, according to custom, he must go and call on each member of the appointing committee. He hated doing so. Shyly he rang the door bell, asked for the member, was shown in and sat down, but when the member came, Pierre was so shy that he praised his rival and not himself in the most glowing terms. Naturally, when the day of election came, it was the rival who was elected.

But something had to be done in order to live. Pierre was able to add to his salary by obtaining a humble post of £100 a year as tutor at the *Polytechnique,* one of the two most famous schools of France.

Just as he did this, the University of Geneva offered him his very heart's desire, a lectureship at the university, a beautiful laboratory, all the instruments and equipment he chose to ask for. He accepted and he and Marie went to Geneva. But when they got there, they knew that they could not desert Paris, could not, simply could not, abandon Radium, that child of theirs. However badly Paris treated them, only in Paris could they work at Radium. So with apologies, Pierre abandoned his wonderful post at Geneva and returned to Paris, poverty and Radium.

We next find the two rejoicing because Pierre had obtained a post in the School of Physics, Chemistry and Natural Science and Marie one to teach girls in the Sèvres training school for elementary teachers. They were lucky young women who had Marie Curie to teach them, but it was sad that the world did not realise that the work she was doing on Radium could only be done by her, while many people might have taught Science at Sèvres. Marie prepared her lessons with the greatest care and won much praise, because they were the most original and the most fascinating lessons any of the girls had known. But her long tram rides several times a week tried her and wasted precious hours; so did the preparation of schoolgirl lessons and the weary marking of papers. It was like setting Rembrandt to paint gate-posts. Both Pierre and Marie were wearing themselves out. Would they ever see Radium?

Marie also had forgotten her good resolution to feed well after her marriage. "You scarcely eat, either of you," wrote their doctor to Pierre. "I have more than once seen Madame Curie nibbling two thin rounds of sausage and washing it down with a cup of tea. Do you think that even a strong constitution won't suffer from such starvation? . . . I know what your excuse will be: 'She is not hungry and is old enough to know what is good for her.' She isn't! She's behaving like a baby. I am speaking with all the conviction of my friendship. You don't spend enough time on your meals. . . . You mustn't read while you eat, or talk Physics . . ."

One gets the impression that neither Pierre nor Marie paid the slightest attention to the doctor's good advice. There was that Radium to be brought to life in the shed of the Rue Lhomond and nothing else mattered.

At one moment Pierre suggested that they should devote themselves to a study of the properties of Radium and abandon the effort to see the thing itself, but Marie would not listen.

She was getting nearer. She had ceased to boil down the rough dust. She had obtained from it something which could be kept indoors, something which, in a small space contained all the Radium of the many tons. To work upon it further, she needed delicate instruments, a science room in which there was neither dust nor damp, neither cold nor heat, nothing to upset an accurate experiment. But she had no such room, and dust, heat, cold, wind constantly undid what she did and forced her to waste time and energy doing it again. She had terrible patience.

It was the year 1902. Three years and nine months had passed since Marie had announced the probable existence of Radium. At last she had conquered the radiant stranger. She had seen stars in that dust; she had seen Radium. She had made one decigramme of it. It had weight. It had the atomic weight of 226. Chemists bowed to it.

Marie and Pierre were sitting at home in the evening and Irène had been put to bed. That four year old tyrant had consented to shut her eyes and let Mé go back to Pierre to finish making the tyrant's dress, for Mé made all Irène's clothes. Suddenly Marie put down her work: "Let's go back!" she said.

Pierre needed no asking. They had left their Radium only two hours but they longed to see it again. They wanted it as if it were a new baby. They called to Grandfather Curie that they were going out and then, arm-in-arm, through the crowded streets, past the factories of their unfashionable district, they made their way back to Rue Lhomond and their shed.

"Don't light up," said Marie. "Do you remember the day when you said you would like Radium to have a beautiful colour?"

In the dark of the shed, Radium had something even more lovely than colour. It had light!

"Look! look!" whispered Marie, as she felt her way to a chair and sat gazing round her.

There were tiny points of light in the dark room, like pale blue moonlight dancing on water, specks of light that were never still. On the table, on the shelves were those strange, mysterious radiances. In its little receptacles there was Radium visible at last, visible by its own light in the dark.

CHAPTER XIII

Not for Sale

THE whole world was excited! Something entirely new had come into people's everyday life, something that made them change their thoughts about many things. It was not only scientists who talked about Radium: children discussed it on their way home from school; women, who had been disappointed for long, long ages because men had made all the greatest discoveries, rejoiced aloud, that at last it had happened to a woman to discover a new and wonderful thing. But, at first, no one dreamed how wonderful Radium was going to be.

Letters came in packed masses to the two Curies from famous scholars in England, Denmark, Germany and Austria, asking for information about the new discovery. Scientists everywhere took up the study of Radium and found out more about its characteristics and those of its near relations. Two Englishmen, Ramsay and Soddy, found that it threw off from itself tiny quantities of a new gas, which they called Helium. In other words, Raduim had the capacity of becoming Helium. That was something very startling. Scientists had been accustomed to laugh at the Medieval Alchemists who believed that they could turn iron into gold. A picture of the alchemist's mysterious smoky cave was a picture of a dream of the impossible. Things, the scientists had said, were themselves, with their own chemical composition and their own atomic weight. Now they had to face the fact that Radium made Helium out of itself, and they wondered what other things might also be occupied with creating new substances. Perhaps the ghosts of the alchemists were laughing at the chemists.

At any rate, to turn iron into gold was no more remarkable a feat than the feats of which this Radium was capable. It looked like dull table salt, but it was two million times more radiant than Uranium. The rays that it gave out could go through every solid metal except lead. It was accompanied by its shadow—a spirit that was so alive and active that even when it was shut up in a glass tube, it destroyed a quarter of itself in a day. It could produce heat of itself, enough heat to melt in an hour a piece of ice of its own weight. If you shut it away from the cold, it would grow hotter than the day. If you shut it in glass, it would turn the glass mauve or violet. If you wrapped it in paper or cotton wool, it ate them. If you had no candle in the dark, it gave you enough light to read by.

One of the most wonderful things about this Radium was that it did not even stick to its own light; it handed it on to everything that came in its way, even though such generosity was often most inconvenient.

It showed a sudden interest in human affairs in

that it lent its luminosity to real diamonds, but turned its nose up at paste. Diamond buyers could use it to test the genuineness of their purchases.

Poor Marie found its interference in all her experiments most distracting. Nothing could be left near a tube of Radium without becoming radio-active; it presented its luminosity to the air, the dust, Marie's clothes, her instruments, her notebooks. Those last kept the luminosity they had not been able to refuse, long after she was dead.

Scientists probably enjoy having their ideas upset, so those early years of the baby Radium must have been happy ones for them. Not only did that strange Radium create a new element out of itself, but that new element again made something new, and so on. The radio-elements formed strange faculties in which each member was created by the transformation of the substance of its mother. But the scientists' shocks did not end there. They found that each radio-element lost half of itself in a given time, a time which was always the same, a time so long that we need not worry about finding ourselves bereft of the radio elements. Uranium, to lose half of itself, takes a few milliards of years, and a milliard is a million-million. To do the same thing, Radium takes only 1,600 years, while its spirit takes only four days and its spirit's children only a few seconds.

You could look at Radium and see it lying quite still and yet know that, while you were gazing at it; its strange children were being born, were being murdered or committing suicide, or merely colliding with one another.

Then suddenly something altogether new happened to this active stranger as if enough things hadn't happened already. Pierre, exploring still, let it burn him. The skin of his hand became red but didn't hurt. It became red.. On the twentieth day a crust formed as on an ordinary fire burn. Then a sore appeared. On the forty-second day the sore began to heal on the outside edge.

Then Marie, though she had not meant to burn herself, found that her Radium had burnt her, though it was in a glass tube and the tube was in a tin box.

Then their friend Becquerel, going home with a tube of it in his jacket pocket, was quite seriously burnt.

"Your abominable child" he exclaimed to Marie. "What has it burnt me for? I love the thing, but I've a bone to pick with it." Marie, too, might have had a bone to pick with the thing she loved, because the tips of her fingers hurt horribly and lost their skin.

But soon people began to look kindly on Radium's burns because they healed so well. Doctors became immensely interested in it. They set it to burn away terribly sick skin and, when the burn was healed, the illness had gone too. A wild great hope began for the world. Perhaps Radium could be persuaded to burn away cancer.

At any rate, Radium had been proved to be useful. People were wanting to buy it. Marie, out of eight tons of pitchblende had made one gramme of Radium. It was worth £30,000, but it was not for sale. Marie would treasure it while she lived and leave it to her laboratory as a precious symbol of years of great work and a great triumph.

One Sunday morning as Pierre and Marie were sitting at home in the Boulevard Kellerman, the postman left a letter with an American stamp for Pierre. He read it carefully, folded it, and put it on his desk.

"We'll have to talk," he said, "about this Radium. It is going to be manufactured on a large scale. They have written from Buffalo to ask for information about it."

"Well?" Marie was a little bored.

"Well, we can choose. . . . We can describe quite openly and frankly all our results and methods of making it. . . ."

"Of course," smiled Marie.

"Or," went on Pierre, paying no attention to the interruption, "we can consider ourselves as the owners of our knowledge, the inventors of Radium. If we do that, before we publish our method of extracting Radium from pitchblende, we must take out a patent and draw a profit from the manufacture of Radium in the whole world."

As he spoke, it was quite clear to them both that immense wealth was theirs for the accepting. A patent on the manufacture of Radium would give them enough money to build a great laboratory and to buy Radium for research. What things they could do if they were rich!

Marie thought for a little, and then said: "That is impossible; that would be against the spirit of science."

Pierre agreed, but he told her to think carefully, because the decision once made could not be reconsidered. He reminded her about the laboratory they both wanted and about the future of their daughter. Was she sure she did not want to be rich?

Marie knew the great old custom of the scientists, the custom that people like Pasteur had followed, and she said: "Physicists always publish their researches. It is only a chance that our discovery has a money value. We can't use a chance like that for profit. And Radium is going to help the sick. It seems impossible to me to seek any profit from it."

Again Pierre agreed that it would be contrary to the scientific spirit to sell their knowledge of Radium. He wrote that very night and gave the Americans all the information they wanted.

So, without a moment's regret, Pierre and Marie turned their backs for ever upon the millionaire's faery fortune. Their Radium was not for sale. The scientific spirit had given Radium to them and to the world, and however low the spirit of the world sinks, it still loves the scientific spirit which gives all its knowledge freely to all men without price. Having chosen poverty when they might have chosen fortune,

Marie and Pierre took their bicycles and went for their ordinary ride through the summer woods to gather wild flowers for their room.

CHAPTER XIV

Darkness

MARIE and Pierre were famous. France offered them prizes. England sent them an invitation. They carried from France a gift for their English friend, Lord Kelvin, a gift of a tiny particle of radium in a glass phial, which he showed with childish glee to his scientific friends. Pierre was to lecture on Radium to the Royal Institute, and Marie was to be the first woman ever to be admitted to a meeting of that severe and splendid Society. Never had there been so gay a lecture there, for Pierre made the wizard Radium show its strange tricks to the solemn assembly of all the most learned Englishmen. The Royal Society was enchanted, and all London was agog to see the two "parents" of radium. There were banquets in their honour, and the noble and the rich glimmered in pearls and diamonds as they gazed in astonishment at that strange thing—a woman scientist, who dined at night in a simple black dress unrelieved by a single jewel, and whose hands, scarred with acids, were bare of any ring; but she looked no less distinguished than they, with her thin figure, her inspired face, and her great pale forehead over those intense eyes. Marie, herself, loved the glitter around her, but she was a little surprised to see the usually in-

different Pierre apparently absorbed in the dazzling scene.

"Aren't jewels pretty things?" she asked him.
"I never dreamed such lovely ones existed."

Pierre laughed. "Do you know," he said, "at
dinner I hadn't anything to do with my mind so I
spent the time working out how many laboratories could h ve been built and equipped with
the price of tl ose jewels!"

No! The Curies were certainly "different."
They understood a substance that gave out its
own light, but not jewelled reflectors. They didn't
even know what to do with a gold medal when
the Royal Society honoured Marie with the Davy
Medal. Pierre gave it to Irène as a thoroughly
safe and biteable plaything, and she adored it.

They knew still less what to do with fame and
crowds and applause and journalists. Marie could
only be miserable about them.

On December 10th, 1903, she was awarded
half the Nobel Prize for Science. Henri Becquerel
had the other half. She was the first woman to be
thus honoured in science, but not a word of excitement escaped her. She rejoiced in the *real* part
of the prize: the recognition by her fellow-
scientists of her work and the gentle pleasure of
having some money to spend; but the glitter and
the tinsel, fame, letters of congratulation from
strangers, demands for autographs, requests for
interviews from photographers and journalists—
those things she hated. "I would like to bury myself to get a little peace," she wrote.

She enjoyed spending the money, and how she spent it showed her in all her sincerity and charm. She banked some of it, so that the family income from it might pay someone to help in the laboratory and also enable Pierre to give up his teaching at the School of Physics and so have time to do research. She gave a large gift to the sanatorium which the Dluskis had founded in Poland. She gave presents to Pierre's brother and her own sisters; she paid subscriptions to scientific societies; she helped some Polish students, her laboratory boys, and a Sèvres girl who was in need. Then she remembered an old French teacher of her own who lived in Poland, who had a lovely, impossible day-dream—that of visiting just once again her dear France. Marie wrote to her, sent her the money for her journey, and invited her to come and stay with her. The old woman wept with joy at the immense unexpected pleasure. Last of all, Marie gave herself a present—a modern bathroom in her house in the Boulevard Kellerman, and new paper for one of her sitting-rooms.

But oh! The foolish crowd! Instead of collecting money to build a laboratory so that the Curies might find out more about Radium, they wasted Marie's time, forced her to play hide-and-seek in the street in order to get into her own house unmolested; published in the newspapers all the little details of their home-life that the Curies loved and would have liked to keep to themselves, even the baby-words that Irène said to her nurse, even the colour of the roof cat. Marie exclaimed,

"They prevent our working. Our life is spoilt
with honour and glory!" And she meant it. She
was shy, and very busy, and the senseless crowd
was making her really ill. Once, when the Curies
were dining with the French President, a lady
went up to Marie and asked if she should present
her to the King of Greece. "I don't see the neces-
sity," said Marie, gently, and then perceived, in
an overwhelming glance. that the lady was Mme.
Loubet, the wife of the President, and that she
was very surprised indeed. "Of course . . . of
course, naturally I'll do anything you like," she
stammered, blushing. To meet kings is a pleasure
to so many people, but Marie was different. She
was tired and she was young. She wanted a holiday, just to be gay and free and happy, and to be
an ordinary mother and an ordinary wife. She
wished Irène's whooping-cough wouldn't take so
many months to go away and that Pierre's illness
wouldn't frighten her. Since she had danced in
Poland twenty years before, her life had been
nothing but work, and never had she so longed to
do nothing, to forget that she was the famous
Mme. Curie, and to be mere Manya again and
eat too many strawberries and sleep and do
nothing.

But Pierre was in a hurry. There was so much
work to do. He couldn't understand Marie's holiday spirit—that was something altogether too
girlish, altogether too unscientific. They must
devote themselves to science, he told her, and she
obeyed. She always obeyed him. But she was

terribly tired, so tired that she almost didn't want her new baby, Eve. "Poor little thing," she said, "to have to live in so hard a world as this." It was indeed a cruel thing that the hunters and pursuers should have taken all her gaiety and courage, even from Manya.

But Eve did her good, for she loved very new babies, and she was obliged to have the month's holiday that Eve gave her—Eve, with the dark hair and blue eyes, who was so different from Irène, of the fair hair and hazel eyes. Eve wouldn't lie in her cradle, but protested vigorously, and Marie was not a model mother who left her to cry, but a soft-hearted one who took her up and carried her about till she slept.

Just before the coming of Eve, an odd privilege had been granted to Marie by the University of Paris, the right to work in Pierre's laboratory. She had been working there all the time, but suddenly the University woke up and gave her an appointment which allowed her to do so—the appointment of "Physics Organiser" under M. Curie at a salary of £96 a year. The University acknowledged, what everyone else had known for a long time, that the Curies always worked together. All their time and their thoughts and their work were quite naturally shared, just as if they were one happy person.

In June, 1905, Pierre and Marie went to beautiful Stockholm, where Pierre had to make a speech, in both their names, in connection with the Nobel Prize. He described Sweden rather

charmingly, as composed of lakes and fjords surrounded by a little dry land, and the two enjoyed
the uncrowded calm of the vast spaces and the
courtesy of a nation which did not press upon
them.

But Marie sometimes made friends with
strangers. There was an American ballet dancer,
Loïe Fuller, who used strange lighting to make
her dancing more beautiful. She wrote to Marie
to ask how she could use Radium to light her

butterfly wings. Pierre and Marie laughed at the wild idea, but wrote back very gently explaining the queer thing that was Radium. Loïe replied that she had only one way of thanking them for their letter—to come and dance to them in their own home. The Curies accepted that uncommon thanks, and on the day there appeared at their door an odd-looking girl with baby-blue eyes and an army of electricians. All day the electricians worked. By the evening the Curies' dining-room was transformed into a fairyland of strange lights, and Loïe danced, making herself by turns flame, flower, bird, and witch.

The little music-hall dancer became a great friend, and took the Curies to introduce them to her friend, Rodin, the great sculptor, and there, in his studio, among the casts and marbles, Science, Sculpture and Dance would sit and talk the evening out.

Then came April, 1906. The hot sun of April in France drew their scent from the violets, purple and white, that coloured the hedgerows in the valley of the Chevreuse. Marie and Pierre, Irène and Eve, were on holiday. In the evening they fetched the milk from the farm; Eve, the little mountebank, making them all laugh as she tottered in the dry cart-ruts. In the mornings, Pierre and Marie, on their bicycles, hunted flowers through the woods and revisited the pond, which they had met on their honeymoon. It was dry and the water-lilies had gone, but yellow-flowering reeds circled the mud with a bright startling crown. And Marie and Pierre, wandering home, gathered violets and powder-blue periwinkle from the banks of the sunken lanes.

At noon on another day they lay in the sun and dreamed, while Irène chased butterflies with a green net, greeting them with high-pitched cries and squeals of glee.

"Life has been sweet with you, Marie," murmured Pierre.

Then, after dinner, he caught the train to Paris and work, carrying with him the yellow ranunculus they had gathered by the pond. The others joined him the next day, and April, as is the way with April, had turned wet and cold.

The day after Marie and the children came home was April the 19th, 1906—a wet day, with muddy, slippery streets, a cloudy day and dark. Pierre had several engagements in the city; Marie had to get the house in order after the holidays, and many things to do in town. Busily, gaily, she went hither and yon. Six o'clock found her back on her own doorstep, happy to be home again, eager to meet Pierre and to begin another of those delicious evenings working with him at scientific calculations.

She opened the drawing-room door. Three men rose and stood, with deep respect in their attitude; just that, as if she had been a queen; and in their eyes she read a terrible pity. Paul Appell, her old teacher, had to tell her that Pierre had slipped in the street and the wheel of a heavy horse-drawn dray had crushed his head.

"Pierre is dead? . . . dead? Really dead?" she said.

When Eve grew up, she told us, in the lovely life she wrote of her mother, that from the moment she spoke the words "Pierre est mort," a cloak of solitude and secrecy enveloped Marie, and that from that April day for ever she was a person apart and lonely.

CHAPTER XV
Whatever Happens

MARIE was born to have glorious courage. All her life she had had to call upon her valiancy, and it had grown strong and would not fail her. Moreover, she had truly loved a great man, and Pierre had left her a word to remember and to obey when her world fell to pieces around her. "Whatever might happen," he had said, one day when they were talking of death, "whatever might happen, and even though one might be like an empty body, whose spirit was dead, it would be one's duty to go on working all the same." So Marie, fortunately, had to go on working. When a pension was offered her, she refused it, saying she was young enough to earn for herself and her children.

She found an odd little way of comfort which seems to make her all the dearer to us: she wrote her diary as if she were speaking to Pierre:

"They have offered to let me take your place, my Pierre: your lectures and the direction of your laboratory. I have accepted. I don't know if I have done right or wrong. You have often told me that you would like me to give a course of lectures at the Sorbonne. And I would at least like to try to continue your work. At one moment that seems the easiest way to go on living; at another I seem a fool to undertake it."

"*May 7th*, 1906:

"My Pierre, I think of you all the time; my head is bursting with the thought of you, and my reason fails. I can't understand that I have to live without you and that I can't smile at my dear life's companion. The trees have been in leaf two days now and the garden is beautiful. This morning I was admiring the children in it. I thought how beautiful you would have thought them and that you would have called me to show me that the periwinkles and narcissus were out. . . .

"*May* 14*th:* I want to tell you that they have nominated me to your chair of Physics at the Sorbonne and that there are people imbecile enough to congratulate me on it." Marie was not too crushed to feel fierce rage at fools.

No woman had ever had the honour of a university chair at the Sorbonne; that is, no woman had been made head of a teaching staff in any subject. But there was no man in France capable of taking over Pierre's work, so it fell naturally to Marie. She alone of living scientists had the genius for it. She determined that her lectures should be worthy of Pierre, so she sent the children to the country and stayed all summer in Paris working on Pierre's subject, on Pierre's notes.

She needed another house and decided to go and live at Sceaux where Pierre was buried. The children's grandfather was a little scared that, when she moved to a smaller house, she would not want him. How could he ask the question?

Marie was also a little scared that he would not want to live with a mere daughter-in-law now that his son was dead. The old man tackled the difficult question: "Now that Pierre isn't here, Marie, you have no reason for living with an old man. I can quite well go and live with my eldest son. It is for you to decide."

"No, you must decide," Marie whispered. "If you go, you will grieve me. But you must choose what you prefer."

"What I prefer, Marie, is to stay with you always."

But the day had to come when Marie would have to go outside her home again where everyone treated her grief with tenderness and respect, and face the outside world where she was now an exciting and famous widow. She knew that the newspapers were asking the Sorbonne to change its rules and make her lecture in the great amphitheatre so that many thousands might hear the first woman to lecture in the Sorbonne. She was probably glad that the Sorbonne was one of the most conservative places on earth and was not likely to change its rules. She had heard that the fashionable crowd, that wished to be present, were discussing what she would say and how she would refer to her husband, because it was the university custom for every new holder of a chair to praise his predecessor. It was the custom to thank the Minister, to thank the university. When the day of its inaugural lecture came, the crowd was waiting, like birds of prey, to hear

Marie say something moving, perhaps to see her break down. It was the small amphitheatre, but they thronged it, crushing the real students who were there to learn, even pushing them out of their seats.

Marie entered quickly amid deafening applause. As soon as there was silence, she began her lecture in advanced Physics simply at the place where Pierre had left off: "When we consider the progress which has taken place in physics during the last ten years, we are surprised at the change in our ideas concerning electricity and matter. . . ."

The audience was surprised indeed, but at the change in their ideas about something other than electricity. They had gone to see a show; they found themselves meeting a woman, who was no show, but a truly sincere human being who thought more about her work than about herself. They were touched. Tears welled up into their eyes. Marie spoke of the new theories of the structure of electricity, of the disintegration of the atom and of radio-active bodies. At the end of her lecture, which was addressed purely to the students, she left the hall as quickly and as simply as she had entered it.

If her work had been hard before, it became harder. She had to think out how to educate the little girls. She had her work of discovery in the laboratory and her lectures at the Sorbonne. She had her house and garden to see to and, above all, she had a special work of her own to do. She had by some means to get a laboratory built in honour of Pierre, something wonderful and perfect it was to be—the laboratory of his dreams.

Eve and Irène played with their blue-eyed grandfather in the new house at Sceaux. He taught Irène botany and natural history and poetry, and helped her to dig her own garden patch and to plant the right flowers, while Eve made friends with her pet tortoise in the grass or romped with the black or with the tabby cat.

But Marie hastened early in the morning, with that quick, business-like step of hers, to catch the Paris train and did not return till the lights were lit in the evenings. The children did not see much of their mother, but it was she who planned the day the children spent. They had to work for an hour at the beginning of the morning. Irène loved figures and Eve music. After that, they went for a walk in all weathers and then to gym, which they loved. Then they cooked or modelled or sewed or gardened or, on a Saturday and Sunday, or in the holidays, they went out bicycling or swimming with their mother. She meant them to be strong and fearless. They were not allowed to be afraid of the dark or of accidents or of climbing, or of riding, or of animals or of anything. Brave and bold they should be and French. She taught them Polish, but she did not want them to have the unhappiness she had had of feeling themselves part of two nations and one a sad and persecuted country. Only one thing she left out of their education—the art of welcoming strangers and being charming at parties. In those things, they had no practice.

Marie did not want her children overworked and hours in French schools are very long, sometimes six hours at school followed by three hours' homework. Marie and her university friends often talked on the subject and they decided to pool their children and teach them themselves. It was a glorious idea Those lucky children were to have one lesson a day, but it was to be given by the greatest specialist in Paris. On the first morning they were to go to the Sorbonne laboratory where Jean Perrin taught them chemistry. "The Sorbonne hasn't yet been blown up," said the newspaper, "but we haven't yet lost all hope." On the next day they went into the country to be taught mathematics by Paul Langevin; on the next to the sculptor, Magrou, to learn modelling; on another to a professor of modern languages and literature, and on Thursday afternoon to the School of Physics to be taught by Marie Curie. Lucky brats!

In that stately place which had never before heard an easy lesson, they dropped inky bicycle bearings on sloping white boards to see with their own eyes the curves that falling bodies make. Or, Marie asked them such dark questions as: "What must I do to keep the heat in this liquid in this pan?"

"Wrap it in wool," said one.

"Isolate it," suggested another.

"I," smiled Marie, "would begin by putting on the lid."

Unfortunately however, parents have to be busy earning the family income and have no time to give their own children enchanting lessons. Those delicious lessons ceased, and Eve and Irène went to school where the hours were not quite so long as in most schools. They said in after-life that from those early lessons they learnt to like work, to be indifferent to money and to be so independent that they were convinced that they could pull themselves out of any difficulty.

In the laboratory, among many new triumphs, Marie had one very great triumph. Up to that time she had made only the salts of Radium. On one occasion she and André Debierne succeeded in making Radium metal. They succeeded once. Neither they nor anyone else has ever done it again.

In 1911 Marie was awarded the Nobel Prize for Chemistry. No person before her had ever received two Nobel prizes.

One would have thought that all the world would have gloried in her as a scientist and treated her gently as a sad woman. But, unfortunately, there is a strange disease which causes certain people to feel very cruel when they hear of someone being very successful or very beautiful. Marie was both, and suddenly people began to write her anonymous letters and to tell extraordinary lies about her and to accuse her of doing wrong things of which she had never dreamed.

Her friends tried to protect her; but it is difficult to fight against enemies who hide. They felt that the best protection would be for the Academy of Science to give her an open honour by making her a member. It was her due, but no woman had ever been a member. The liars redoubled their efforts to prevent the election. They even went the length of putting a false voting paper into the hand of a blind man, her friend, so that he might seem to oppose her. The Academy of Science, to its lasting disgrace, rejected her by one vote.

Marie was terribly unhappy about the lies. For a time she had to borrow her sister's name to escape from her enemies. She was as open as the day and this attack from the people who skulked in darkness made her ill. It almost destroyed that famous courage of hers, but not quite She was very ill and in great pain. The surgeons said an operation would save her from pain, but she told them to wait till after she had attended the next Physics Congress. Her courage was still there.

Then when she was still ill there came to her a great decision to make. She was tired and wanted not to have to think, but Poland had decided to build a great laboratory of radio-activity at Warsaw, and invited her to be the head of it. How she longed to accept! What an invitation it was! She was told that Poland needed her, that her country was growing discouraged and needed something to make it believe in itself again.

But long years before Marie had decided that greatly though she loved Poland, she loved Pierre

Curie more. She still loved him more, and Poland and he were still pulling in opposite directions. If Marie gave herself to Poland, she would have to give up the hope of building Pierre's laboratory. Without her presence in France, Pierre's dream would never come true. She refused Poland sadly.

But Poland insisted that she should direct the new laboratory from a distance and go to the opening of the new building. Many exciting things befell her during that visit. First, she gave an address on Science in Polish, and it was the first time in her life that she had ever used her own tongue for a scientific speech. Secondly, she attended a great ceremony in the museum where she had done her first Physics experiments. Thirdly, at a banquet given in her honour by Polish women, she discovered the old headmistress of her first school. Hurriedly, Marie made her way through the crowd to the old lady and kissed her on both cheeks. What joy that old headmistress must have felt at the thought that her "old girl" was without question the most famous woman!

Marie had earned a holiday. She was going to spend it walking in Switzerland with a rucksack on her back and teaching Eve and Irène to climb and to treat crevasses with proper respect.

They had a friend with them who talked Physics so enthusiastically with Marie, that the children had to keep watch over him lest he, not they, should fall into a crevasse. They listened with surprise to the odd things he said to their mother, and laughed so much that there was no one to look after the crevasses.

"You see, Madame," they heard him say, "what I need to know is: what exactly happens to the passengers in a lift when it falls in a vacuum?" The question seemed easy to answer to Eve and Irène and very amusing. They did not guess that they were listening to that incomprehensible subject called "Relativity," for the careless friend was none other than the great Einstein.

At that time, Marie was becoming happier again, because the walls of Pierre's Radium Institute were growing in the Rue Pierre Curie. Dr. Roux, the head of the Pasteur Institute, had proposed two years before to raise the money for a laboratory for Madame Curie. That made the Sorbonne wake up to the fact that the Pasteur Institute was thinking of snatching their Madame Curie from them, and, to prevent such a catastrophe, they agreed with the Pasteur Institute to share in the building of the new laboratory.

Marie was full of joy. She helped to make the plans, discussed the shape of all the rooms and windows with the architect, and insisted on having immense windows and overflowing light. She also insisted on a garden and planted the trees and roses with her own hands before the building began, so that they might be making a little show when it was opened.

In July, 1914, she was able to read on the stone over the door:

Institut du Radium Pavillon Curie.

She tells us that she thought of Pasteur's words: "If you care for those conquests that are useful to men . . . if you are jealous of the part which your country may claim to have played in the spread of these marvels, take an interest, I implore you, in these sacred dwellings which we call laboratories. Ask that their numbers be increased, that they may be splendid. They are the temples of the future, temples of true wealth and well-being. It is in them that man grows great, grows strong, and grows good. There he learns to read the works of Nature, which are the works of progress and universal peace; while his own works are too often barbaric and destructive."

So thought Marie Curie, remembering Pasteur, as she watched Pierre's completed Institute of Radium, in July, 1914. The building was ready, but Marie would have to wait four years, four years of war, before she could see work begin in the Institute of Radium and Pierre's dream come true.

CHAPTER XVI

War

August 1st, 1914.
"Dear Irène, dear Eve,

"Things seem to be going from bad to worse: we are expecting mobilization at any moment—I don't know if I shall be able to get away. Keep cool, be brave and calm. If there is no war, I shall come on Monday; if war comes, I shall remain here and send for you as soon as possible. Irène, you and I must try to make ourselves useful."

August 2nd.
"Mobilization has begun and the Germans have entered France without a declaration of war. It will be difficult to get letters through for some time.

"Paris is calm and impressive in spite of the grief for the men going to the Front."

August 6th.

"Brave little Belgium has not agreed to let them pass through without fighting. Everybody in France is hopeful that the struggle, though hard, will end in victory.

"Poland has been occupied by the Germans. What will remain of my country when they have finished with it? I have no news of my family."

So wrote Marie to the children, who were on holiday in Brittany.

In Paris, Marie was extraordinarily alone. All her fellow-workers had gone to the war except one mechanic who had heart-disease and could not join up. Marie was ill and weak. But it did not enter her head to think of that or of the catastrophe that was happening to her work. She did did not follow the crowd of women who were offering to be nurses. As she had always done, she thought quickly and fiercely: where was there a gap to be filled with her work? The hospitals at the front, the hospitals behind the lines, were almost without X-ray appliances, were without that almost new and magic device by which a surgeon could see through men's flesh the shot or splinter of shell sitting fixed in the depths of a wound. X-rays had never been any business of Marie's; she had only been interested in them and had had a few lessons on them. That didn't matter. She would, with all speed, create X-ray stations. It took her only a few hours to make a list of all the X-ray apparatus available in Paris and get it distributed to the hospitals. Then she collected any scientists who could or would use it, and distributed them also. Paris was provided for.

But the wounded, pouring back, pouring back in their thousands, in ambulances from the front to field hospitals, what was to become of them? Marie did not hesitate. Time was everything. She turned for money to the U. F. de F.—the Union of the Women of France—and produced the first "Radiologic Car." It was an ordinary motor-car with the electricity for the X-ray run off the engine. That travelling X-ray station went from hospital to hospital in the poor, shattered, beautiful Marne country, enabling all the wounded of the greatest battle of the war to be quickly examined, safely operated on, and many, many of them to be saved, who without it would have died.

But before the battle of the Marne the Germans were fighting only a few miles from Paris. Would they get through? Would they take Paris? What ought Marie to do? Her children were alone in Brittany. Ought she to go to them? Ought she to go with the medical corps when they evacuated Paris? No. She was going to stay in Paris, whatever happened; because, as she put it, "*Perhaps* if I am on guard in the new buildings of the Pierre Curie laboratory the Germans will not dare to sack it; whereas if no one is there, for certain they will leave nothing." Headstrong, unyielding Marie hated the mere thought of any flight. To be afraid was to help the enemy. Not for anything in the world would she give the enemy the satisfaction of entering a deserted Pierre Curie Institute! But if Marie wasn't leaving Paris, her one precious gramme of Radium had to go, and there was no one to escort it but herself.

She put on her black alpaca dust coat, packed her night things, and with a small, extraordinarily heavy packet of lead, took train for Bordeaux. Cramped on a wooden bench in the crowded train, with her Radium at her feet, she gazed out of the window at the fields under the burning early September sun and at the roads crowded with unending cars and carts fleeing always, fleeing to the west.

At Bordeaux, on the far western sea, Marie stood on the platform, hour after hour, with her little packet of lead still at her feet, the packet which was too heavy for a woman to carry and too valuable to be left alone. There were no porters and no taxis and no bedrooms. She smiled as she wondered if she would have to stand there all night. But she was rescued at last by a fellow-traveller, who helped to find her a bed and to house the Radium safely in a bank.

On the next morning she returned to Paris. In the evening she had been an unnoticed traveller in a mighty crowd of safety seekers, but in the morning she was stared at by a crowd who had collected to see the strange marvel of "the woman returning up there!" The woman returning up there was glad of the chance to tell them that there was no danger "up there," that Paris would not fall, that its inhabitants would be in no danger.

The woman returning up there, however, was hungry. She had had nothing to eat since the night before, and the troop train she was on merely crept towards Paris when it wasn't standing at ease in the fields. She was very glad of a bit of bread a friendly soldier gave her out of his haversack. And then when she reached lovely, threatened Paris, the joyful news came out to meet her that the enemy was held on the Marne.

Without a moment's rest, Marie rushed to the headquarters of the "National Help Society" to see what next she should do.

"Lie down, woman!" exclaimed its President, Appell, "Lie down and rest." She obeyed, but only while she discussed her future work. "With those great eyes of hers in her pale face," said Appell, "she is nothing more than a flame."

Then came the turn of the "little Curies." Marie had two children in Brittany, but to the soldiers of France she was mother to the X-ray motor-cars that soon began to meet them everywhere as they were brought wounded from fighting. Marie fitted those cars out one by one at the laboratory and wrung from unwilling officials all they needed. She who had once been timid, bearded any lion in any den on behalf of her little Curies. She extracted "passes" from one, "passwords" from another, visas from another—money from the rich, smart motor-cars from the kindly—"I'll return them," said she, "if they are still returnable at the end of the war—I will indeed."

L

A big Renault, more like a lorry than a car, she took for herself. Then began a life of outdoor adventure.

In her room in Paris the telephone bell rang. A big convoy of wounded needed an X-ray station. She went out to her car, painted grey for war with a big red cross; she carefully checked over her apparatus; then, while the soldier chauffeur filled up, she put on her dark coat, with red cross arm-band, and her soft, round, faded hat, and climbed into the seat beside the driver, with her old, yellow, cracked and sun-scorched leather bag. And then, at all the speed the slow old car could muster, she went, wind-whipped or rain-whipped, in the day or in the night, and without lights, into the war at places whose names are known for the fierceness of the fighting—Amiens, Ypres, Verdun.

Sentinels stopped them, enquired, passed them. The Renault found the hospital. Madame Curie chose her room and had the cases carried into it; then rapidly she put the apparatus together while others unrolled the electric cable that connected the car's dynamo with the apparatus. The chauffeur started up and Marie verified the current. Then she placed each thing in its right place, her protective gloves and glasses, her special pencils and lead wires for localising metal; then she darkened the room, with curtains if there were any or with bedclothes if there weren't. Meanwhile a second room had been got ready as a photographic dark room.

In half an hour from the time of her arrival, everything was ready, including the surgeon. Then began the long procession of the stretchers with the wounded; one after the other, one after the other, men in great pain, they came. Marie arranged her apparatus; the surgeon looked and saw among the shapes of bones or organs a dark fragment of this or that.

Sometimes an assistant wrote notes about the position of the metal at the surgeon's dictation for a later serious operation. Sometimes then and there the surgeon was able to operate and watch, while he worked, his pincers advancing into the wound and getting round some part of the bony skeleton to seize a piece of shrapnel.

The hours, and sometimes the days, passed. As long as there were wounded, Marie stayed in the dark room. Before she left the hospital, she had made her plans for installing a permanent X-ray theatre in it. In a few days, having moved heaven and earth to get it, she returned with the new apparatus and a new radiologist, whom she had conjured from nobody knew where.

In that way she personally installed 200 X-ray stations in hospitals, which, with her twenty cars treated more than a million wounded. That was great work for one woman.

But we mustn't fancy her, when she drove, always sitting beside a chauffeur in luxury on her front seat, protected from the weather. There were times when she had to do the driving and swing the mighty starting handle. She could congratulate herself when she hadn't more than two punctures, in a journey on those roads covered with splinters of every kind. She was often changing wheels with those same delicate, radium-burnt fingers in the terrible frost and wet that marked the war years. Sometimes she might be seen frowning a scientist's frown as she cleaned, most scientifically, an unfamiliar carburettor. Sometimes she was doing porter's work, lifting heavy cases, when all men were in the fighting line.

Once she was angry! Her chauffeur, taking a curve too quickly, upset the car into a ditch and buried Marie under all the loose cases. Not that Marie mattered. It was the thought of what had happened to her delicate apparatus that made her furious. But she laughed aloud from under the cases when she heard the young man running round and round the car trying to catch a glimpse of her and asking, "Madame, are you dead? Madame, are you dead?"

Sometimes she forgot her breakfast or her dinner. Always she slept anywhere—in a bed if she could get one, under the stars if only they were available. It was natural to her, who had lived hard in her youth, to find herself a soldier of the Great War.

But that soldierly work was not all Marie's work. When she had time, she packed all the instruments in her old laboratory and had them taken to Pierre Curie's new laboratory. There she unpacked them and gradually fitted out the new home of science. She went to Bordeaux and

brought back her gramme of Radium, and every
week she "drew" its emanations from it, enclosed
them in tubes and sent them for use to the
hospitals.

With the tremendous increase of X-ray work,
radiologists were needed. Marie taught and
trained them in the new Radium Institute. Some
of them were stupid and clumsy and hard to
teach; but with infinite patience and sympathy
she encouraged them and helped them, till they,
too, could make a success of the delicate work. In
that teaching she was helped by Irène, who was
17 by then. Irène had been studying radiology
while still at the Sorbonne, and her mother had
not thought her too young to work in the war
hospitals.

In two years they trained 150 radiology nurses.

As if all that were not enough, Marie visited
Belgian hospitals. Sometimes in hospitals where
she was a stranger, fashionable ladies, who were
nursing, mistook the shabby, poor-looking
woman for a cleaner and treated her with scant
courtesy. Marie didn't mind; she only felt more
warmed and comforted by the charm of a certain
nurse and a certain silent soldier who contentedly
worked with her at d'Hoogstade: Elizabeth the
Queen and Albert the King of the Belgians. She
herself had lost all her cold distant manner and
was just charming and infinitely gentle and en-
couraging with the wounded soldiers. She used
to explain to the ignorant, scared peasants that
her strange apparatus would not hurt them any

more than a camera would. She was gay again.

She never spoke of herself, never said she was feeling tired, never felt frightened of shells falling round her. With all that work she went on daily, as if it were the most natural thing in the world.

But she longed for peace, longed for all that mad cruelty to come to an end! For her, with all the rest of the world, November 11th, 1918, was the happiest day that had been, when the cannon shot that marked the Armistice surprised her in her laboratory. Instantly she rushed out with her assistant, Mlle. Klein, to buy flags that the Institute might join in the glory. But there wasn't a flag in Paris! They had to make do with lengths of three colours which they sewed together. Then Marie took the old Renault and joined the wild throng in the streets, reckless of the fact that she had ten uninvited passengers on the wings and on the roof.

Who can guess the joy of the days that came after?

For Marie, it was not only her France that was free from the overwhelming terror, but her Poland also. Poland at last was free and independent. She wrote to her brother:

"So we, 'born in servitude and chained in our cradles,' have seen the resurrection of our country."

CHAPTER XVII

At Home

MARIE was at home again in a big old-fashioned flat on the Seine Quay side. The Seine has two islands in the heart of Paris: the *Ile de la Cité*, the ship-shaped isle, the oldest part of Paris, the old, with its sombre, beautiful and famous buildings; and the *Ile St. Louis*, old too and more lonely, where Marie lived on the *Quai de Bethune*. Two centuries before, the houses in the Rue de Bethune had been inhabited by dukes and gentlemen of the court. Marie's flat was a rambling place of corridors and many stairs. Her rooms were immense and lofty and empty. She had never learnt how to be rich or how to draw comfort around herself. Her few pieces of mahogany furniture stood about anyhow on the wide spaces of the slippery polished floor! She and Irène shivered and didn't notice it in the icy cold and bareness, but Eve spent her pocket money on attempts to make her own huge den cosy and elegant. One room was beautiful, Marie's study with its severe bookcases, its portrait of Pierre and its vase of flowers; and all the rooms had the beauty of light, for the windows were high and curtainless and they looked out on to the view that all the artists paint: the broad sunlit Seine with its busy little ships and colourful heavy barges and the towers of Notre Dame in the distance.

Marie had chosen the island for its loneliness and its quiet, but she seemed not to mind that, in fact, her house was full of noises. Eve's scales resounded on the piano hour by hour, a cat woke the echoes galloping down the corridors, the door bell clanged and the telephone rang through the emptiness, while the raucous syrens of the tugs came in from the river.

By eight o'clock every morning Marie's energetic, rapid footsteps, warned Irène and Eve that the busy day had begun. Any day for the next sixteen years was something like this: At eight-forty-five three blasts of a motor horn told Marie that her little car was at the door. She hastily snatched her hat and coat and ran downstairs, because she would never think of keeping her chauffeur waiting more than three minutes. She began by having the handy man at the Institute to drive her, and when she took to a regular chauffeur, the poor man wept for grief that someone else should drive Marie. She drove across the Tournelle bridge and across the busy quays to the Latin quarter, where from the beginning of history, gay and rowdy students have lived in proverbial happiness and poverty and where, now-a-days, all the great learned institutes and buildings stand.

In the Rue Pierre Curie, Marie found herself at the entrance to the Institute of Radium. There was a crowd in the hall. Every morning there was a crowd in the hall and Marie called it the

Soviet. Her students from this or that department always came to catch her before she went
to her work, so that they should not trespass on
her time, they said. They had a particular question to ask her or something to show her; or they
hoped that Marie, overnight, had got out a problem for them. She often had. "Oh, Mr. So-and-
So, your solution wouldn't work, but I have
another for you. . . ." Marie turned from one
difficult piece of work to another, the crowd increased, each one bringing a difficult conundrum.
Marie seemed not to mind what mental gym-
nastics they expected of her. Problems were
often put to her in broken French or broken
English, which added to the difficulty in hand.
The Institute was quite a tower of Babel with
all the languages of the East as well as all the
tongues of the West. Marie tells a tale of her
Chinese student who talked with her in English:
he was so polite that even when she was wrong
and he knew it, he had to agree with her and she
had to use the very best of her brain to *guess* the
silent contradiction which was at the back of his
mind. She said that she was ashamed of her own
manners in the presence of her Eastern students:
"They are so much more civilized than we."

The hall session often seemed unending and
Marie would have to sit to it and, as there were
no chairs, to sit on the stairs. It is a charming
picture to think of her squatting on the lowest
stair teaching her tall students at their feet. She
was chief of the laboratory; she had read every

book on anything to do with Radium in five languages; she was still inventing new techniques; she seemed to work by magic; her pupils could trust her guidance entirely. She was both bold and prudent.

One by one the students would go off to their particular experiments. Perhaps one who had something to show would take Marie with him; perhaps she would at last find herself free to go to her own laboratory and do her own work.

At mid-day she walked home to lunch but she still discussed Physics at the table with Irène. Eve sometimes felt out of it. Her mother and sister talked of *BB prime and BB squared* and as, in French, BB is pronounced *bébé*, which means baby, Eve was left wondering what a squared baby and a prime baby could possibly be.

But, in 1926, Irène married a brilliant young scientist called Joliot and Eve had the conversation to herself.

"Darling, you do the talking," said Marie. "What are they doing in the world?" And Eve would talk to her about everything, for everything interested her, especially simple and childish things. She liked to hear how fast Eve drove, or what the baby said, when Irène's baby began to say things, or what people thought of the new Fascists.

"Ah!" said Marie, if by chance anyone praised a dictator, "I have lived under oppression. You haven't. You don't understand how happy you are to live in a free country." And if anyone upheld the right of a Government to kill a rebel, she said: "You will never convince me that to guillotine Lavoisier served any purpose."

After lunch the car would fetch her again and perhaps she would go to the flower market to buy her common garden flowers or wild ones if she could get them, for she never liked smart, green-house things. Or perhaps she had an appoint-ment in the Luxembourg gardens with a very important personage, her baby granddaughter, Helène. She would sit and play at making sand-pies with her till it was time to go to the after-noon's session of the Academy of Medicine. There Marie was the only woman and her seat was next to her friend Dr. Roux, who had been Pasteur's most devoted disciple.

After the Academy, Marie went back to the laboratory and worked till dinner time on ordin-ary days; but sometimes till 2.0 in the morning if her experiments needed it.

Sometimes the seriousness of the place was disturbed by a tea party given in honour of some student who had become a doctor of science. Then scientific glasses became tea cups and glass rods served as spoons and the party closed with an address by Marie in which she congratulated the new doctor. The two happiest of those teas were those which celebrated Irène's doctorate and that of her husband, Frédéric Joliot. In 1934 those two made a great discovery, nothing less than *artificial* radio-activity. They bombarded aluminium and other substances with the rays of

Radium and transformed them into new radio-active substances which had never been known before and which became sources from which Radium could be drawn. Scientists saw that a time might come when substances could be manu-factured to do the work of Radium the rare. What a wonderful thing that would be, for across the garden, opposite the Radium Institute, was the building in which Radium was helping to cure cancer by the method known as Curie-therapy. Radium was necessary and Radium was very rare.

Then there were the letters. Think of the letters of an important person! Fortunately a secretary opened the thousands of them—letters from thoughtless people asking for autographs, which they didn't get; letters asking foolish questions; letters from advertisers, from beggars. And in the great piles just a letter here and there that needed an answer.

Lastly, Marie had her lessons to give. Those were the things she hated. On a Monday and a Wednesday she was sick with nervousness from dawn till five o'clock, because she had to stand in the little amphitheatre and address some thirty students at once.

In those years she was threatened with blind-ness. The doctors told her that she must put up with being nearly blind for two or three years till she could have an operation. Probably they never dreamed what that meant to her. She wanted to work and she hated sympathy. Whatever happened, she did not want other people to know about her eyes. Eve had to book her glasses at the oculist's as those of Madame Carré. If she had a student's paper to correct, she made him bring it to her and then answer cleverly put questions on it, so that in that way she knew what he had written. She thought of every clever device to conceal her misfortune and the people who guessed pretended to notice nothing. That was to be truly kind. After her four operations she had to teach her eyes to work again. They would never work as they had worked, but her courage did not fail; she made them work.

But let us get back to Marie's day. We left her having late dinner with Eve. After dinner Eve had to go out and Marie, who was tired, lay on her sofa and watched her daughter dress. "Horrible heels, Eve! You will never make me believe that women were made for walking on stilts."

"And what's this new fashion of bare backs? Bare in front is bearable, but these kilometres of bare back! Still the dress is pretty enough. Turn round and let me see how pretty you are." Marie looked at her daughter with consternation: "I haven't any objection on principle to all this daubing. I know it has always been done. In ancient Egypt women invented worse things. I can say only one thing: I think it is hideous. You are cruel to your eyebrows and you daub your lips for no reason."

"But, Mé, I really look better so."

"Better! ! ! Listen, to console myself I shall come and kiss you in bed to-morrow morning before you have had time to put these horrors on your face."

When Eve had gone, Marie, in her armchair, read a little poetry or a few pages of a favourite novel, but not for more than an hour. The floor was her place—the floor that gave her room to spread all her Physics papers around her and to work out her problems till two in the morning.

So Eve found her mother when she came in, a mother so absorbed in work that she did not notice her but went on counting, half aloud as she used to do at school and in Polish.

CHAPTER XVIII

Abroad

IT was May, 1920. The sun was hot. The chestnuts in Paris were all in bloom, and Marie was, as usual, working. But an event was about to break in on her work; a most surprising event that she didn't expect in the least.

Marie never saw newspaper men, still less newspaper women. She hated being interviewed; she hated publicity. She had neat slips printed to say politely and firmly to strangers who wanted to meet her: "Madame Curie regrets. . . ."

But people with Irish names who live in America sometimes have an odd little way of finding a right, irresistible word, and there was a certain Mrs. Meloney who had written to Marie: "My doctor father always used to say that it is quite impossible to exaggerate the littleness of human creatures. But for twenty years you have been great in my eyes, Madame, and I want to see you, only for a few minutes." That was another way of saying: "Might a very little cat look at a queen?" and Marie, breaking all her own rules, said "Yes."

So Mrs. Meloney waited on that May morning in Marie's tiny waiting-room at the Radium Institute, and this is how she described what happened:

"The door opened, and I saw come in a pale, timid woman with the saddest face I have ever seen. She had on a black cotton dress. Her splendid, patient, gentle face had the absent-minded look of people who study much. Suddenly, I felt that I was a mere intruder; I became even shyer than Madame Curie. I had been a professional reporter for more than twenty years and yet I couldn't manage to ask a single question of this defenceless woman in black cotton."

It was Marie who set the reporter at ease by talking about America and Radium. She told her that America had fifty grammes of Radium, and she knew exactly how many grammes were in each town. "And how many has France?" asked Mrs. Meloney. "My laboratory possesses a little more than a gramme."

"You have only a gramme of radium?"

"I? I haven't any. This gramme belongs to my laboratory."

Then Mrs. Meloney began to speak of patents. She imagined, she said, that Marie must be drawing much money from those who used her methods of producing Raduim.

"Radium ought not to enrich anyone," said

Marie. "It is an element. It belongs to everybody."

Mrs. Meloney must have felt then that the whole world ought to give Marie a present in return for what she had given the world. She said suddenly, "If you could choose out of the whole world the thing you would have, what would it be?"

Marie hesitated, "I need," she said, "a gramme of radium to go on with my researches. But I can't buy it. Radium is too dear for me."

It was then that Mrs. Meloney determined that America should give Marie Curie a gramme of Radium. She went home and tried to persuade ten rich women to give £3,000 each. But she could find only three. Then she turned from the few rich to the many poor. All the women of America should join together to give Marie the gift. In less than a year she wrote to Marie: "We have the money. Your Radium is yours."

But America had grown excited over the collection. Soon all the girls and women had heard of the *Madame Curie Radium Fund;* everyone wanted to see Madame Curie. But Marie hated crowds. She did not want to go, but she had never before been offered so lovable a gift. Still she began to make excuses. She couldn't be separated from her daughters. That didn't worry hospitable America; they invited the girls, and told Marie that the gramme of Radium would be presented to her by the President himself.

So Marie, Irène and Eve packed all their

clothes into one single trunk and set sail in the *Olympic's* most luxurious cabin, for America willed it so. France gave them a great send-off with a gala performance at the Opera, in which the greatest actors, Sarah Bernhardt, and the famous Guitrys, took part. Only the Atlantic refused to join in honouring Science; the ocean remained morose, dark and uncivilised, and encouraged Marie to dream with longing of the blue sunlit seas at home.

As the *Olympic* docked, Mrs. Meloney, who had travelled with her, brought Marie from her cabin to meet a real American welcome, and only those who have experienced it can imagine the warm-hearted sincerity of it. The crowd had been waiting five hours to greet her whom they named, "The benefactor of the human race." It was summer; the skies were blue above the splendid white skyscrapers. The quay was colourful with the flags of Poland, France, and America. Students, girl-guides, three hundred women representing the Polish women of America, waved red and white roses before her. She sat, rather like a child trying to be good, in an armchair on the upper deck, while Mrs. Meloney took away her hat and her handbag and posed her for the photographers. "Your head to the right, please, Madame Curie." "A little more this way please . . . !"

America went mad with welcome. The Americans were determined that the world should see through their eyes that a scientist is perhaps the

greatest human-being. Their hearts were captured
by Marie's love for pure science, by her scorn of
profit, and by her conviction that to serve is the
true purpose for which men live.

Nothing that they could invent to honour her
was neglected. They wanted to welcome her
everywhere and forgot the long distances of their
great country. They offered her banquets where
the guests were five hundred, and forgot the long
hours. They offered her titles of honour by the
bagful, and forgot that in her own country she
refused them all. They asked her to university
ceremonies and were surprised that she had no
cap and gown. They offered her flowers grown
especially for her, and forgot that she preferred
them wild. Love is often like that; but Marie,
though tired, understood. The only thing she
could not tolerate was the magnificent university
gown they made for her, for to expect her to wear
silk was just a little too much, because silk irritated her fingers that Radium itself had injured.

Marie's first visits were to the women's colleges.
Everywhere she went, girls in white made hedges
to the roads or ran in immense clusters across
fields to greet her carriage. And above the white
masses were always the coloured streamers of the
flags. At an immense gathering in New York the
university women passed in long file before her,
bowing and presenting alternately the Lily of
France and the Rose of America. In another
gathering of ambassadors and the great of many
lands, at which she was given the "Freedom of

New York", the most famous person after herself was Paderewski, whom long ago, when he was a struggling pianist, she had encouraged with her clapping.

Then came the great event: the presentation of the gramme of Radium.

The White House at Washington was prepared for the fête. The President of the United States and all the great people of America were there to meet Marie, but Radium itself was absent. It was too dangerous and too precious to sit about on tables and be handled by a president. It stayed safely in the factory and was present only by proxy. On a table in the east room during the ceremony stood a Radium casket containing tubes of imitation Radium.

At four o'clock the double doors were thrown open and the procession entered, Marie on the arm of President Harding.

In his address, the President reminded the guests that Marie was not only a great scientist, but a devoted wife and mother. She had done the daily work of a man and all her womanly duties in addition.

At the end of his speech, he gave her a rolled parchment, the deed of gift, and hung the tiny gold key of the real casket round her neck. Then, in the blue room, Marie sat while all the guests passed in procession before her and shook hands with Irène and Eve, because she herself was too tired.

So Marie possessed a gramme of Radium! By

no means. On the evening before the ceremony, Mrs. Meloney had shown her the deed of gift and she had insisted, then and there, though it was late at night, that a lawyer should be sent for to give the gramme legally to her laboratory. When Mrs. Meloney suggested that the week after would do, Marie exclaimed: "I might die to-night!" From that evening her gramme was just something to work with which belonged to the laboratory.

There were other visits to make. America, full of penitence at having tired its guest, tried to spare her fatigue in every possible way. Sometimes they arranged for her to arrive at the station before the one at which she was expected, and when the excited people found out what had been done, there was a stream of cars along the road to meet the traveller. Sometimes Marie had to get out of the train on the wrong side, jump down to the rails and walk across them, which could not have been really restful. Sometimes Irène and Eve were accepted as their mother's understudies, and nobody smiled when staid professors spoke to sixteen-year-old Eve of her "magnificent discoveries" and "her lifetime of labour."

But Marie was present herself when the Poles fêted her in Chicago. To them she was a symbol of their distant birthplace and her triumph was Poland's. Men and women, their faces wet with tears of joy, tried to kiss her feet or the hem of her dress.

On the *Olympic*, on which she sailed home at

the end of June, was the Radium itself, locked in behind the complicated locks of the ship's safe. But in her letters, it was not of Radium she wrote, but of a little touch of gladness in her heart because she had been able to win just a little more American friendliness for France and Poland.

America's joy in her had taught Marie how much she meant to the great world. She realised that her mere name, her mere presence, could help the things she cared for and loved. So she began to travel more and face ceremonies and congresses. She became known the world over. She visited South America, Spain, England and Czecho-slovakia. Even in China, though she did not go there, there was a portrait of her in a temple of Confucius side by side with the Buddhas and the Emperors of the Celestial Empire.

In all her travels she enjoyed the odd things she saw. She liked the fish that jump out of the water and fly through the air and, at the Equator, it amused her that she lost her shadow, and she loved the wild flowers, new and old, that met her in strange places.

But apart from the things that she merely looked at and loved, there were the other loved things that she journeyed to fight for. Like every-one else who had served mankind, she hated war. She had been willing in war to do a soldier's work in defence of her country; but in peace, she was eager to serve in preventing future wars. She refused to take time from research to belong to

Societies, but she made one exception: she allowed herself to be nominated by the Council of the League of Nations as a member of the society of men and women who decided to use their brains to find ways of getting different nations to work together. That Society was called "The International Committee on Intellectual Co-operation." Marie did not belong to it merely to talk. She set to work to do definite things. One was to get scientific people of all nations to use the same scientific terms and to make complete lists of all the scientific books and discoveries all the world over, so that every student could know what work had already been done.

Next, Marie wanted a scheme to help any scientific genius who might, in any nation, be too poor to develop its gifts. It is horrible waste, she thought, to throw away a genius. She gave all her strength to help to create a world in which freedom, peace and science were ever more and more. Now that the Radium Institute in Paris was working, Marie determined to build a Radium Institute in Warsaw. Her sister Bronia, who was in Poland, launched the appeal. All Poland was soon covered with placards; all the post-offices sold stamps with Marie's picture; postcards invited everyone to "buy a brick to build the Marie-Sklovodska-Curie Institute," and, on them in Marie's writing, were the words: "My most ardent desire is the creation of a Radium Institute in Warsaw."

In 1925, Marie was able to go to Warsaw for

the foundation of the Institute. The President of the Republic laid the first brick, Marie the second. Laughingly, he asked her if she remembered the travelling pillow she had lent him when he was poor. She replied: "Yes, and you forgot to return it." She remembered, too, that the famous actor who complimented her from the stage was none other than Monsieur Kotarbinski, for whom Manya had once plaited a crown of wild flowers.

But a Radium Institute was a queer place without Radium. Mrs. Meloney had again to persuade the United States to give Marie another gramme, and again Marie went to New York. On that occasion it was to thank the Americans in the name of Poland. She stayed at the White House and found it very amusing to see it full of elephants, large elephants, small elephants, minute elephants, white elephants. As a parting gift she was given two elephants, a little ivory one and an almost invisible one. Elephants were the badge of the governing party. With her two and the Radium, she returned to Warsaw to see the Institute begin its work of curing the sick.

As she had done when she was a little girl, she wandered by the great Vistula and wrote about it: "The river winds, broad and lazy, gray near at hand and blue as heaven in the distance. Adorable sandbanks, sparkling in the sun, show here and there and mark the capricious course of the stream. At the edge of these banks, strips of more brilliant light show where the waters grow deep. I simply have to wander by these light-filled magnificent shores. . . . There is a song which says: 'In this Polish water there is such charm that those who love it once, love it for ever.' To me that is true. This great river has a deep inexplicable fascination."

CHAPTER XIX

Holiday

THERE was a place in Brittany. Pink granite cliffs and rocks ran out into a blue, clear sea that was always calm, because a reef of a thousand islands kept out the Atlantic tumult of the waves. There, in a dip among the rocks was Larcouëst, a group of fishermen's cottages, not even a village, a mere hamlet, where the Breton fishwives went out and in with their wide, white linen bonnets protecting their faces from the wind.

High up on the moor, in the clear path of all the winds and looking like a lighthouse, was Marie's little holiday home, a wisp of a little poor cottage with a glorious view. Marie was a nobody in Larcouëst. The king of the country was a little old hunchback man with smiling eyes behind spectacles, and the palace where he lived was a long, low cottage covered from ground to roof with virginia-creeper, wild red fuchsia, and travellers' joy. It stood in an orchard and was called Taschen-Vihan, which in Breton means "the little orchard field." Its door was always open, except when the east wind blew, and all the old king's subjects—Marie and Irène and Eve and Frédéric Joliot and children and babies and scientists and writers—in fact all the people who loved him and everybody loved him, visited him all day

long and never gave a thought to the fact that
he was one of the most learned historians who
ever lived, none other than Charles Seignobos
whom everybody knows. He had discovered
Larcouëst, and every summer the wisest, most
learned people of Paris went to make holiday
there.

Every morning, Marie in a washed-out linen
hat, an old skirt, sandals and the black reefer
jacket that all Larcouëstians wore, fishermen and
ladies alike, used to take the steep path that led
hither and thither down from her moor and ended
among the flaming flowers of Taschen's garden.

"Good-morning, Madame Curie," called
Seignobos.

"Good-morning!" echoed the fifteen or so
others who were lying about in the grass or the
flowers, looking, in their queer rig-out, like a
company of gypsies.

Marie slung her rucksack on the ground and sat
beside it. Larcouëst, like everywhere else, had its
severe social distinctions; but they were of a
different kind from those in most villages. In
Larcouëst people of the lowest rank were called
Philistines. They were simply strangers who
didn't belong to Larcouëst. Next above them
came the people whom you could just know, the
Elephants. They were friends, but unfortunate
landlubbers, people who were not as comfortable
in and on the sea as they were on the land. They
were to be pitied, but they could be improved.
Above them came the honourable of the place, the

Sailors, and then in distant, worshipable dignity, were the *Crocodiles,* those to whom all the arts of the sea were known. Not only could they swim, they could "crawl" and manage sails and oars among the stiffest currents. Marie had never been a Philistine and had little hope of ever being a crocodile. She had begun as an elephant and had risen to be a sailor.

At a word from Seignobos, the sailors of the day loosed from the fleet of two sailing boats and six rowing boats which were moored at the quay, the pinnace and the dinghy, and sculled them to the rock landing-stage.

"Aboard! aboard!" ordered Seignobos. "I'll row stroke, Madame Curie will row bow; Perrin and Borel to the oars, and Francis, you steer."

The crews were all professors. The white and green boat went round in a circle, for one pulled too hard. The steersman called his oarsmen to attention: "Bow is not following stroke." Marie blushed and timed her stroke. The sea rippled under the sun, and the mariners sang:

> Three little boys sail for the isles!
> Who sail with a boat-load of joys
> For the isles, are three little boys. . . .

At the end of the third song, it was time to change the oars because stronger rowers were needed to take the boats through the current to Roch Vras, the violet-coloured desert island where the Larcouëstians bathed. The men took as their dressing-room the shore which they shared with the brown gulls; the women had a rock chamber carpeted with soft green grass.

Marie was first into the deep transparent water. She was a good swimmer even if she could not do the crawl. In the water she was young again, her gray hairs were hidden under her cap, and no-one could see her wrinkles. She was slender and graceful and quick and deliciously proud of her skill. "Aren't I much better than Borel?" she called to Irène, and Irène, who was no flatterer, could truthfully answer: "Oh *much* better, Mé. There is no comparison."

After the bath, Marie sunbathed and ate a crisp little loaf. "It's a good life," she would murmur, or, "Isn't it lovely?" No-one, not even Marie

Curie, was allowed to say anything more about the beauty of Larcouëst. It was one of the things that were not done. Larcouëst was the loveliest place in the world. Everybody knew it and so it was not necessary to say so.

At mid-day the boats went home to the songs of the crews. Marie, bare-foot and bare-legged, her sandals in her hand, picked up her skirts and waded to the shore through the black mud where the white gulls sat in crowds.

The company lunched in their own homes, but most of them returned to Taschen at two to sail in the yacht *Wild Rose*. The yachts and the boats all belonged to Seignobos. Everything belonged to him, but he was one of those people who liked their possessions to be the property of all their friends. Marie did not sail; she found sitting in a sailing yacht too slow an occupation. Instead, she sat at home in her lighthouse correcting science papers; or she took her spade, her fork and her secateurs and gardened. Her reeds and brambles drew her blood; her unexpected rocks twisted her ankle, or she crushed her own fingers with her hammer; but she paid no attention to small matters. At six she bathed again and went to Taschen to keep the oldest old lady company and watch for the return of the *Wild Rose*. Its sails, golden in the setting sun, appeared just before dinner, and its wild happy crew came back to Taschen, the girls' hair decorated with the carnations Seignobos gave them each day from his garden.

After dinner everyone went back to Taschen through the ever-open door. Perhaps they played games, simple games like word-making or charades. Sometimes there was a ball. An accordion played the music for old-fashioned dances, and everybody danced together—scientists and peasants, servants and masters.

Sometimes on fine nights, Marie and Irène and Eve went arm-in-arm for walks in the dark along mysterious, winding paths by the wine-dark sea. Did some sudden wind, bringing the booming of great breakers from beyond the reefs, remind Marie that, like the sea, her Radium was radiant yet dangerous? Larcouëst is near to Paimpol. The Larcouëstians played all day with a sunlit sea; but the men of Paimpol were the men of the Iceland fisheries who knew best the dark and bitter strangeness of the sea.

Every year in her holidays Marie played with the glittering, innocent sea. In her worktime, she played with Radium. She breathed in its rays. It burnt her hands, for she disdained the leaden shields which she made other people wear. It did strange, mysterious things with her blood. It puzzled the greatest doctors of France.

It was not till one summer day, July the 4th, 1934, when Marie Curie lay dead of an unknown illness at Sancellemoz in the mountains, that the doctors guessed that she had died from too great friendliness with her great discovery, Radium.